SALMAGUNDI

SALMAGUNDI

BYRON, ALLEGRA,

AND THE TROLLOPE FAMILY

BY

N. JOHN HALL

BETA PHI MU

1975

Beta Phi Mu Chapbook Number Eleven
Published by Beta Phi Mu, Pittsburgh, Pennsylvania
Copyright N. John Hall

*Library of Congress
Cataloging in Publication Data*

Hall, N   John.
  Salmagundi: Byron, Allegra, and the Trollope family.

  (Beta Phi Mu chapbook; no. 11)
  Includes the text of a ms. transcribed by Anthony Trollope bearing the title "Salmagundi—aliena, 1834," which contains Mrs. Trollope's poem "Lines written by a celebrated authoress" and 3 short anonymous poems. Also included as an appendix is Mrs. Trollope's verse-drama "Signs of the times; or, The righteous rout."

  Includes bibliographical references and index.

    1. Trollope, Frances Milton, 1780-1863. 2. Byron, George Gordon Noel Byron, Baron, 1788-1824—Biography. 3. Trollope family. 4. Clairmont, Allegra, 1817-1822. I. Trollope, Frances Milton, 1780-1863. II. Title. III. Title: Salmagundi—aliena, 1834. IV. Series: Beta Phi Mu. Chapbook; no. 11.

PR5699.T3Z7   821'.7 [B]   75-1156
ISBN 0-910230-11-0

CONTENTS

ILLUSTRATIONS

PREFACE

With Chapbook No. XI, Beta Phi Mu enters its twenty-third year of publishing books which have at least approached, if not met, the objectives of the society's founders. The original purposes of this national honorary fraternity were defined as recognition of academic achievement in library science and the sponsoring of professional and scholarly projects which would contribute to the general field of librarianship. Among the latter has been the publication of this series, which is meant to contribute not only to the literature of books and librarianship but equally to the art of book design.

N. John Hall, author of this lively and fascinating introduction to Frances Trollope's previously unpublished satiric poem, earned his Ph.D. in English literature at New York University in 1970. Since that date he has been assistant professor at Bronx Community College, City University of New York. An authority on Victorian literature, Dr. Hall has published Anthony Trollope's survey of mid-Victorian life (*The New Zealander*, Clarendon Press, 1972), and several articles relating to Trollope. He is at present editing a new edition of Trollope's letters for Stanford University Press.

Designer for this chapbook is P. J. Conkwright, art editor for the University of Oklahoma Press from 1929 to 1939, and book designer for Princeton University Press from 1939 until his retirement in 1970. During the latter period, fifty-three of the books he designed were chosen in the American Institute of Graphic Arts annual "Fifty Books of the Year," the largest number so placed by any single designer. A native of Oklahoma (Creek Indian country near Tulsa), Mr. Conkwright studied at the Chicago Art Institute and the National Academy of Commercial Art, is a graduate of the Universities of Kentucky and Oklahoma, taught graphic arts at Princeton, was winner of the American Institute of Graphic Arts Gold Medal in 1955 and the Frederic W. Goudy Award in 1974, and is a member of the American Academy of Arts and Sciences, Grolier Club, and Newcomen Society of North America.

FOREWORD

THE subject of this small book, if it can be said to have a single subject, is a manuscript tucked away among the Trollope family papers in the University of Illinois Library. It bears the curious title, "Salmagundi—*aliena*, 1834" and has been endorsed on the title-sheet by Anthony Trollope as "My mother's lines on the burial of Lord Byron's illegitimate daughter." That Mrs. Trollope wrote such a poem has long been known, but all trace of it was thought to have perished. Nevertheless, the poem survives, a 500-line satire upon the Harrow Church Vestry for its refusal in 1822 to allow a commemorative tablet over the tomb of little Allegra Byron. But the small 5½ by 8½ inch manuscript of thirty-two pages (sixteen single sheets folded once and sewn together) turns out to be more than a copy of Mrs. Trollope's long-thought-lost satire. The "Salmagundi" or potpourri of four poems is entirely in the hand of Anthony Trollope, written at the age of nineteen. As such it is the earliest extant manuscript of any kind from his pen. Two of the short poems may even be Trollope's own; but of more interest are the numerous and revealing notes Anthony has appended to his mother's poem. This book then has various focuses of interest: Byron and Allegra, the Harrow affair, Mrs. Trollope, and Anthony Trollope.

The text given for the "Salmagundi" poems follows Trollope's manuscript precisely, except for minor regularization of punctuation, the writing out of abbreviations and ampersands, and the correction of a few errors ("grew" for "crew", "too" for "two") that were obviously the result of hasty copying. Anthony Trollope's footnotes are indicated by daggers, as in the manuscript. My notes are numbered or asterisked and printed in small type.

I wish to thank Mr. Lucien W. White and the University of Illinois Library for permission to publish the manuscript. To Professor Gordon N. Ray I am especially indebted: he has read through my manuscript and made helpful suggestions; moreover, it was he who in 1953 brought the Trollope papers to the University of Illinois Library. I have also had generous help from the following: Mrs. Helen W. Tuttle, Chairperson of the

Publications Committee for Beta Phi Mu; Leslie A. Marchand, Professor Emeritus, Rutgers University; Professor Wilfred S. Dowden, Rice University; Professors Mortimer H. Frank and Bernard L. Witlieb, Bronx Community College, CUNY; Publisher John Murray; Mrs. Mary Ciebert, University of Illinois Library; Mr. R. G. Morgan, the British Museum; Mrs. Dorothy Lindsay, the National Portrait Gallery; Mr. Paul Sykes, City of Nottingham Library; Mr. C. H. Shaw, Harrow School; Mr. Robert S. Call; and Mr. K. Harris. I acknowledge gratefully a Grant-in-Aid from the American Council of Learned Societies. Particular gratitude is due my wife, Marianne, who has assisted me throughout.

New York 1974   N.J.H.

SALMAGUNDI

BACKGROUND

ALLEGRA

THE life of Lord Byron has attracted as much curiosity as that of any figure in English literary history. Certainly no other poet during his lifetime ever achieved the popularity and notoriety that Byron did. Since that morning in 1812 after the publication of *Childe Harold* when Byron "awoke to find himself famous," critics, essayists, biographers, memoirists, collectors of letters and memorabilia have labored over the incredible person and career of the poet. The early writers fell into two broad categories: those so enthusiastic, adulating, and worshipful as to be willing to suppress what they felt was harmful to his reputation, and those so shocked, outraged, inimical as to be willing to misrepresent and even invent to strike a blow. Only in our century have editors and biographers been able to approach their subject in a more disinterested and objective fashion. And with the wealth of information available, it is not surprising that Byron's natural daughter Allegra, who died at the age of five years and three months, should have a history of her own.

Her story begins in the spring of 1816 at the time of the breakup of Byron's unhappy and short-lived marriage to Anne Isabella Milbanke. While his marriage remained intact—indeed since the year 1812—Byron had been the naughty darling of London society. Now suddenly he found himself enveloped in a scandal which appeared unprecedented even in those scandal-loving days: his wife of one year had left him in January and pressed relentlessly for a deed of separation while London boiled over with rumors of incest, "unnatural acts," and madness. Wounded and disgusted (and pressed for debts), Byron was preparing to leave England for the Continent when he received a letter from an unknown female admirer calling herself E. Trefusis:

> An utter stranger takes the liberty of addressing you. . . .
> If you feel your indignation rising, if you feel tempted to
> read no more, or to cast with levity into the fire, what has

been written by me with so much fearful inquietude, check your hand: my folly may be great, but the Creator ought not to destroy his creature. . . . If a woman, whose reputation has yet remained unstained, if without either guardian or husband to control she should throw herself upon your mercy, if with a beating heart she should confess the love she has borne you many years, if she should secure to you secrecy and safety, if she should return your kindness with fond affection and unbounded devotion, could you betray her, or would you be silent as the grave?[1]

The writer was Mary Jane ("Claire") Clairmont, not yet 18, stepdaughter of William Godwin, daughter of Godwin's second wife by her former husband.[2] Claire, intelligent, well-read for her age, musically gifted, had been reared according to Godwin's freethinking philosophy, as had her stepsister Mary (Godwin's daughter by his first wife, Mary Wollstonecraft, author of *A Vindication of the Rights of Women*). In 1814 Claire had accompanied Mary Godwin and Shelley on their elopement to the Continent, and she was in fact to continue with brief interruptions to live with the couple until Shelley's death.*

When Byron did not reply, Claire persisted; her next letter presented her as a lady who "desires to be admitted alone and with the utmost privacy." Byron then wrote a brief note indicating he would be home to her, but her ensuing letter complained, "I have called twice on you; but your Servants declare you to be out of town"; when she begged his assistance in furthering her ambitions for a theatrical career, he gave her the name of his friend Douglas Kinnaird. She then vainly sought Byron's appraisal of a half-written novel; but what may have helped her cause was her connection with Shelley, whom Byron

* Claire was the inspiration for at least two poems by Shelley, "To Constantia Singing" and "To Constantia." She was also the original for Stella in Thomas Love Peacock's *Nightmare Abbey*. Stella-Claire, who vies with Marionetta (Harriet) for Scythrop (Shelley), has been substituted for Mary Godwin. Peacock gives Stella lines such as "I rely on myself. . . . I act as I please, go where I please, and let the world say what it will. . . . I submit not to be an accomplice in my sex's slavery. I am . . . a lover of freedom, and I carry my theory into practice" (chap. x).

had never met but whose *Queen Mab* he admired. After Claire had managed to visit Byron, she wrote:

> I do not expect you to love me; I am not worthy of your love. I feel you are superior, yet much to my surprize, more to my happiness, you betrayed passions I had believed no longer alive in your bosom. Shall I also have to ruefully experience the want of happiness? shall I reject it when it is offered? I may appear to you imprudent, vicious; my opinions detestable, my theory depraved; but one thing, at least, time shall show you that I love gently and with affection, that I am incapable of any thing approaching to the feeling of revenge or malice; I do assure you, your future will shall be mine, and every thing you shall do or say, I shall not question.
>
> Have you then any objection to the following plan? On Thursday Evening we may go out of town together by some stage or mail about the distance of ten or twelve miles. There we shall be free and unknown; we can return early the following morning. I have arranged every thing here so that the slightest suspicion may not be excited.[3]

From the ten surviving letters (most of them undated) of this initial correspondence the exact sequence of events is not easily discernible. They do establish, however, that Byron formed with this importunate girl the most reluctant liaison of his career. Some few weeks later, when on April 25 he quit England —for ever as it turned out—he was glad to escape from her along with his more pressing troubles. But Claire, in the company of Shelley and Mary Godwin, soon followed him and at Geneva performed her great service to English letters by bringing together Byron and Shelley.

The introduction took place May 27, and by early June both poets had established households near each other at the Lake of Geneva. Claire easily managed frequent visits to Byron's Villa Diodati, and thus Byron, almost against his will, took up again with her. Claire tried to make herself useful, writing out fair copies of a new canto of *Childe Harold* and of *The Prisoner of Chillon*, but as the weeks passed she so bored

Byron that he did his best to avoid her. By the end of August, when she was to depart with the Shelleys, he would not even speak with her. Nor would he ever see her again. Byron described the summer to his half sister Augusta:

> as to all these "mistresses"—Lord help me—I have had but one. Now don't scold—but what could I do? A foolish girl, in spite of all I could say or do, would come after me, or rather went before for I found her here, and I have had all the plague possible to persuade her to go back again, but at last she went. Now dearest, I do most truly tell thee that I could not help this, that I did all I could to prevent it, and have at last put an end to it. I was not in love nor have any love left for any, but I could not exactly play the Stoic with a woman who had scrambled eight hundred miles to unphilosophize me, besides I had been regaled of late with so many "two courses and a *desert*" (Alas!) of aversion, that I was fain to take a little love (if pressed particularly) by way of novelty. And now you know all that I know of that matter, & it's over.[4]

Augusta did not quite know all, for before Claire returned to England she had, in Shelley's supporting presence, told Byron she was carrying his child. He seems from the first to have determined to care for the child himself, although for him the break with Claire was irrevocable.

By January 1817 he was writing to Kinnaird:

> You know, and I believe saw once, that odd-headed girl, who introduced herself to me shortly before I left England; but you also know that I found her with Shelley and her sister at Geneva. I never loved nor pretended to love her, but a man is a man, and if a girl of eighteen comes prancing to you at all hours, there is but one way—the suite of all this is that she was with *child*—and returned to England to assist in peopling that desolate island. Whether this impregnation took place before I left England or since I do not know; the (carnal) connection had commenced previously to my setting out—but by or about this

time she is about to produce—the next question is, is the
brat mine? I have reasons to think so, for I know as much
as one can know such a thing—that she had *not lived* with
S. during the time of our acquaintance—and that she
had a good deal of that same with me.

    This comes of "putting it about" (as Jackson calls it)
and be damned to it—and thus people come into the
world.[5]

Although Byron did not yet know at this time (January 20),
Claire had already given birth to a girl on January 12 at Bath.
Shelley, in whose house the child and her mother remained for
more than a year, wrote to Byron: "Claire is safely delivered of
a most beautiful girl"[6] and in more detail on April 23 he described "a little being whom we—in the absence of all right to
bestow a *Christian* designation—call Alba, or the Dawn. She is
very beautiful, and though her frame is of somewhat a delicate
texture, enjoys excellent health. Her eyes are the most intelligent I ever saw in so young an infant. Her hair is black, her
eyes deeply blue, and her mouth exquisitely shaped."[7] But
Byron selected his own name, Allegra. And by May he was writing to Augusta:

    I shall be glad to hear from or of you, and of your
children and mine. By the way, it seems that I have got
another—a *daughter* by that same lady, whom you will
recognize by what I said of her in former letters—I mean
her who returned to England to become a Mamma incog.,
and whom I pray the Gods to keep there. I am a little
puzzled how to dispose of this new production (which is
two or three months old, though I did not receive the
accounts till at Rome), but shall probably send for and
place it in a Venetian convent, to become a good Catholic,
and (it may be) a *Nun*, being a character somewhat wanted
in our family.

    They tell me it is very pretty, with blue eyes and *dark*
hair; and, although I never was attached nor pretended
attachment to the mother, still in case of the eternal war
and alienation which I foresee about my legitimate

daughter, Ada,* it may be as well to have something to
repose a hope upon. I must love something in my old
age, and probably circumstances will render this poor little
creature a great and, perhaps, my only comfort.[8]

Meanwhile Shelley from his new house at Marlow continued
to send Byron rhapsodic accounts of Allegra:

> [She] is grown exquisitely beautiful, and her temper has
> lost much of its *vivacité*, and has become affectionate,
> and mild. She is [my son] William's playmate, who
> is so fond of her. . . . They sit on the floor together and
> amuse themselves for hours in the most sociable way;
> little William putting more than half the raisins, etc. that
> are given to him into her mouth.[9]

But for all Shelley's love of Allegra, he realized that she could
not remain in his household indefinitely (scandal made Allegra
his child**) and he grew anxious for Byron to claim his
daughter. To Kinnaird Byron wrote:

> Shelley (from Marlow) has written to me about my
> daughter, (the last bastard one), who, it seems, is a great
> beauty; and wants to know what he is to do about sending
> her . . . will you think of some plan for remitting her
> here, or placing her in England? I shall acknowledge and
> breed her myself, giving her the name of Biron (to dis-
> tinguish her from little Legitimacy), and mean to christen
> her Allegra, which is a Venetian name.[11]

* Augusta Ada Byron, born December 10, 1815, the poet's daughter by
his wife, Anne Isabella; Ada married Lord King and became Countess of
Lovelace; she died in 1852, having become (in spite of her mother's efforts)
very devoted to her father's memory.
** Robert Southey, the Poet Laureate, was the source of much of the
scandalous rumor; Byron told Hobhouse: "The son of a bitch on his return
from Switzerland, two years ago, said that Shelley and I 'had formed a
League of Incest, and practised our precepts with, &c.' He lied like a rascal,
for they *were not sisters.* . . . He lied in another sense, for there was no
promiscuous intercourse, my commerce being limited to the carnal knowledge of the Miss C."[10] Byron's indignation at this time inspired his famous
"Dedication" of *Don Juan* to Southey.

By March 1818 arrangements were finally completed for Allegra's transport to Byron at Venice:

> A clerk can bring the papers [wrote Byron to Hobhouse]
> (and, by-the-bye, my *shild* by Clare, at the same time.
> Pray desire Shelley to pack it carefully), with *tooth-powder,*
> *red only*: magnesia, soda-powders, tooth-brushes, diachy-
> lon plaster, and any new novels good for anything.[12]

But in fact Shelley himself brought Allegra to Italy (having first had her baptized together with his own two children). Claire accompanied the Shelleys as far as Milan, but Byron refused to see her or acknowledge any letter from her, and the child was sent on to Venice in the care of the Shelleys' Swiss nurse, Elise.

Allegra arrived in Venice on May 2 and was soon established in Byron's newly acquired Palazzo Mocenigo, along with his domineering mistress, Margarita Cogni ("La Fornarina"—a baker's wife), numerous servants and a grand assortment of dogs, monkeys, caged birds, and a fox. Byron was evidently quite taken with his daughter. He wrote to Augusta:

> My little girl, Allegra . . . is very pretty, remarkably in-
> telligent, and a great favourite with every body; but,
> what is remarkable, much more like Lady Byron than her
> mother—so much so as to stupefy the learned Fletcher
> and astonish me. Is it not odd? I suppose she must also
> resemble her sister, Ada: she has very blue eyes, and that
> singular forehead, fair curly hair, and a devil of a Spirit—
> but that is Papa's.[13]

Byron's fondness for Allegra, however, did not prevent him from realizing that his Palazzo was not a very suitable home for her, and by August she was placed with Richard Hoppner, the English Consul, and his wife. Here Claire, with Shelley's help, made a secret visit to her daughter. Shelley then visited Byron and thus was Allegra instrumental in reuniting the two poets, even as her mother had first introduced them. Out of this visit grew Shelley's *Julian and Maddalo*, in which poem he included some lines on Allegra:

A lovelier toy sweet Nature never made,
A serious, subtle, wild yet gentle being,
Graceful without design and unforeseeing,
With eyes—Oh speak not of her eyes!—which seem
Twin mirrors of Italian Heaven, yet gleam
With such deep meaning, as we never see
But in the human countenance: with me
She was a special favourite: I had nursed
Her fine and feeble limbs when she came first
To this bleak world.

Byron was so softened by his friend that he arranged to let Shelley have his villa at Este where Claire might spend almost two months with her child. By October Allegra was again entrusted to the care of the Hoppners in Venice. The following June Byron followed Countess Teresa Guiccioli (with whom he would form his most permanent liaison) to Ravenna and then to Bologna where Allegra was reunited to him in August 1819. Byron described her to Augusta:

> She is English, but speaks nothing but Venetian. "Bon di, papa" &c &c she is very droll, and has a good deal of the Byron—can't articulate the letter *r* at all—frowns and pouts quite in our way—blue eyes—light hair growing *darker* daily—and a dimple in her chin—a scowl on the brow—white skin—sweet voice—and a particular liking of Music—and of her own way in every thing—is not that B. all over?[14]

When Teresa's husband began to raise serious objections to her behavior at Bologna, Byron contemplated emigrating to South America with Allegra; and after Teresa returned to her husband at Ravenna, Byron reluctantly decided to break with her altogether and return to England. He went to Venice, collected his belongings, including Allegra, aboard the gondola, but then, as a reliable witness testified, declared that "if it would strike one o'clock before everything was in order (his arms being the only thing not yet quite ready) he would not go that day. The hour strikes and he remains. Evidently he had not the heart to go."[15] Soon a call from the Countess' father—Teresa was ill—summoned Byron to Ravenna where at Christmas he became Teresa's acknowledged *cavalier servente*. At Ravenna Allegra was much petted and admired by all and especially by Teresa herself. But Byron's praise of his daughter had by this time grown somewhat qualified: "Allegra is prettier I think, but obstinate as a Mule, and as ravenous as a Vulture. Health good to judge by the complexion, temper tolerable, but for vanity and pertinacity. She thinks herself handsome, and will do as she pleases."[16]

Meanwhile Claire wrote through the Hoppners asking that Allegra spend some of the summer in Pisa with her and the Shelleys. Byron replied to Hoppner:

> About Allegra, I can only say to Claire—that I so totally
> disapprove of the mode of Children's treatment in their
> family [the Shelleys], that I should look upon the Child
> as going into a hospital. Is it not so? Have they *reared*
> one?* Her health here has hitherto been *excellent*, and
> her temper not bad; she is sometimes vain and obstinate,
> but always clean and cheerful, and as, in a year or two,
> I shall either send her to England, or put her in a Convent
> for education, these defects will be remedied as far as they
> can in human nature. But the Child shall not quit me

* An unkind reference to the deaths of three children of Shelley and Mary: the first, prematurely born, died after three weeks on March 5, 1815; Clara, one year old, died in Venice, September 24, 1818; and William, three years, died in Rome, June 7, 1819; another son, Percy Florence, born November 12, 1819, lived until 1889.

Byron's worldly cynicism led him to accept all too readily in August of 1820 the slander that Shelley had had a child by Claire which was placed in a foundling home at Naples. Until told otherwise by Shelley a year later, he believed the story as passed on by the gossipy Hoppner from two dismissed servants of Shelley, Paolo Foggi and the nursemaid Elise. Shelley had in fact registered at Naples in December of 1819 a child named Elena Adelaide as his and Mary's. Mystery still surrounds the parentage of Elena, who died within eighteen months.[17]

One should note Byron's final estimate of Shelley as expressed to John Murray after the poet's death: "You were all brutally mistaken about Shelley, who was, without exception, the *best* and least selfish man I ever knew. I never knew one who was not a beast in comparison."[18]

again to perish of Starvation, and green fruit,* or be taught to believe that there is no Deity.[19]

Claire, increasingly alarmed at Byron's mention of a convent education for Allegra, continued to importune him through the Hoppners, and he grew ever more impatient towards her. He complained to Hoppner:

> Claire writes me the most insolent letters about Allegra; see what a man gets by taking care of natural children! Were it not for the poor little child's sake, I am almost tempted to send her back to her atheistical mother, but that would be too bad; you cannot conceive the excess of her insolence, and I know not why, for I have been at great care and expense,—taking a house in the country on purpose for her. She has *two* maids and every possible attention. If Claire thinks that she shall ever interfere with the child's morals or education, she mistakes; she never shall. The girl shall be a Christian and a married woman if possible. As to seeing her, she may see her— under proper restriction; but she is not to throw every thing into confusion with her Bedlam behaviour. To express it delicately, I think Madame Clare is a damned bitch.**[20]

On March 1, concerned with both Allegra's education and the threatening political situation in Ravenna (where he had allied himself with the revolutionary Carbonari) Byron placed Allegra in the Capuchin Convent of San Giovanni at Bagnacavallo, some twelve miles from Ravenna. The youngest age for admittance to this school was seven, and Allegra, who was only four, was admitted in view of her father's rank and a double fee. Byron did not take Allegra to the convent himself but entrusted this office to his banker friend, Pellegrino Ghigi, whose own daughter attended the school. Byron wrote to Hoppner:

> I have neither spared trouble nor expense in the care of the child; and as she was now four years old complete,

* A reference to Shelley's vegetarianism.
** Claire in her journal refers to Byron as *"my damn'd brute,"* May 1, 1820.

and quite above the control of the servants—and as a
man living without any woman at the head of his house
cannot much attend to a nursery—I had no resource but
to place her for a time (at a high pension too) in the
convent of Bagna-Cavalli . . . where the air is good, and
where she will, at least, have her learning advanced,
and her morals and religion inculcated. . . . It is also fit
that I should add that I by no means intended, nor intend,
to give a *natural* child an *English* education, because
with the disadvantages of her birth, her after settlement
would be doubly difficult. Abroad, with a fair foreign
education and a portion of five or six thousand pounds,*
she might and may marry very respectably. In England
such a dowry would be a pittance, while elsewhere it is a
fortune. It is, besides, my wish that she should be a Roman
Catholic, which I look upon as the best religion, as it is
assuredly the oldest of the various branches of
Christianity.[21]

Claire, her worst fears about the convent realized, sent raging
letters, which Byron ignored. Meanwhile Shelley wrote tactfully:
"Mary, no less than myself, is perfectly convinced of your conduct towards Allegra having been most irreproachable, and we
entirely agree in the necessity, under existing circumstances, of
the placing her in a convent near to yourself."[22]

All evidence seems to indicate that Allegra was not only well
cared for but petted and catered to at the convent. Shelley,
while staying with Byron at Ravenna, made a three-hour visit
to Allegra at Bagnacavallo on August 14. His letter to Mary
the next day is the most detailed picture of Allegra to have
survived:

She is grown tall & slight for her age, and her face is
somewhat altered—the traits have become more delicate,
& she is much paler: probably from the effect of improper
food.—She yet retains the beauty of her deep blue eyes
& of her mouth, but she has a contemplative seriousness
which mixed with her excessive vivacity which has

* Byron had left Allegra £5,000 by a codicil to his will, November 17,
1818.

not yet deserted her has a very peculiar effect in a child.
She is under very strict discipline as may be observed
from the immediate obedience she accords to the will of
her attendants—this seems contrary to her nature; but
I do not think it has been obtained at the expense of
much severity. Her hair, scarcely darker than it was,
is beautifully profuse & hangs in large curls on her neck.
She was prettily dressed in white muslin and an apron
of black silk with trowsers.—Her light & airy figure & her
graceful motions were a striking contrast to the other
children there—she seemed a thing of a finer race & a
higher order.—At first she was very shy, but after a little
caressing and especially after I had given her a gold
chain which I had bought at Ravenna for her she grew
more familiar, & led me all over the garden & all over
the convent running & skipping so fast that I could hardly
keep up with her. She shewed me her little bed, & the
chair where she sate at dinner & the carozzina in which
she & her favourite companion drew each other along a
covered walk in the garden.—I had brought her a Basket
of sweetmeats, & before eating any of them she gave her
companion & all the nuns a portion.—this is not much like
the old Allegra. I asked her what I should say from her to
her mamma & she said—'Che mi manda un *bacio* e un
bel vestitino'—'E come vuoi il vestitino sia fatto?' 'Tutto
di seta e d'oro'* was her reply.—Her predominant foible
seems the love of distinction & vanity—and this is a plant
which produces good or evil according to the gardeners
skill.—I then asked—what shall I say to papa—'Che
venga farmi un visitino, e che porta seco la *mammina*'—
a message which you may conjecture that I was too discreet
to deliver.** Before I went away she made me run all over
the convent like a mad thing—the nuns who were half
in bed were ordered to hide themselves, & on returning

* "That she send me a kiss and a pretty little dress." "And how do you
want the little dress made?" "All of silk and gold."
** "That he pay me a little visit and bring Mama with him." Allegra
may have meant Teresa, rather than Claire, whom Allegra had not seen
since Este when she was less than two years of age.

Allegra began ringing the bell which calls the nuns to assemble, the tocsin of the convent sounded, & it required all the efforts of the prioress to prevent the spouses of God to render themselves dressed or undressed to the accustomed signal.—Nobody scolded her for these scappature: so I suppose that she is well treated as far as temper is concerned.—Her intellect is not much cultivated here— she knows certain orazioni by heart & talks & *dreams* of Paradise & angels & all sorts of things—and has a prodigious list of saints—and is always talking of the Bambino. This fuora will do her no harm—but the idea of bringing up so sweet a creature in the midst of such trash till sixteen!—[23]

In a long postscript, Shelley added that he had persuaded Byron to come to Pisa as soon as a house could be gotten for him. "Our first thought ought to be Allegra,"[24] Shelley added. When the Mother Superior at Bagnacavallo heard of Byron's plan to remove from Ravenna, she wrote to suggest that he visit his daughter before his departure. Her note was on the reverse side of one from Allegra:

Caro il mio Pappa
Essendo tempo di Fiera desidererei tanto una Visita del mio Pappa, che ho' molte voglie da levarmi, non vorrá compiacere la sua Allegrina che l'ho ama tanto?
[My dear Papa As it is fair-time, I should so much like a visit from my Papa, because I have so many whims to satisfy, won't he please fulfill the wish of his little Allegra who loves him so much?]

Byron sent the letter to Sir Walter Scott with the comment: "A propos of Epistles I enclose you two—one from the Prioress of the Convent—and the other from my daughter her pupil— which is sincere enough but not very flattering—for she wants to see me because 'it is the fair'—to get some paternal gingerbread—I suppose."[25] Byron left Ravenna October 29 without seeing Allegra and settled into the Palazzo Lanfranchi, the Pisan house which Shelley had found for him.

In the months that followed, Claire's hatred of Byron and fears for Allegra grew apace, and she formulated wild plans for abducting Allegra from the convent. Shelley discouraged her outlandish scheme, part of which called for Shelley to forge a letter to the Mother Superior of the convent; he pointed out that any such attempt was bound to fail and would, moreover, inevitably lead to a duel between Byron and himself. But Byron's callous disregard of Claire seems to have led Shelley to consider withdrawing somewhat from close friendship with Byron.

Then, suddenly, Allegra died on April 20, 1822. There had been word of a fever for some weeks, but serious danger was never suggested; in fact the most recent communication announced her almost complete recovery. Some doubt remains whether her disease was typhoid or consumptive fever, but she seems to have received good medical attention, including that of Dr. Sante Rasi of Ravenna who had formerly attended her. It fell to Teresa Guiccioli to tell Byron:

> "I understand," said he,—"it is enough, say no more." A mortal paleness spread itself over his face, his strength failed him, and he sunk into a seat. His look was fixed, and the expression such that I began to fear for his reason; he did not shed a tear. . . . He remained immoveable in the same attitude for an hour, and no consolation which I endeavoured to afford him seemed to reach his ears. . . . He desired to be left alone, and I was obliged to leave him.[26]

Byron entrusted to Teresa arrangements for shipping the body to England, and he refused to meet with the men (one of them a priest) who conducted the body to Leghorn. Ghighi recorded:

> They have come back [to Ravenna] much mortified that Mylord would not receive them, and I too blush that it should one day be known (for now we strive to conceal it) that this was so. I too believe that Mylord is very sensitive and much grieved, but I am also aware that every man has his pride—and one must not, on account of one's own grief, forget what is due to others.[27]

To Shelley, Byron confided:

> The blow was stunning and unexpected. . . . But I have
> borne up against it as I best can, and so far successfully,
> that I can go about the usual business of life with the
> same appearance of composure, and even greater. . . .
> I do not know that I have any thing to reproach in my
> conduct, and certainly nothing in my feelings and inten-
> tions towards the dead. But it is a moment when we are
> apt to think that, if this or that had been done, such
> event might have been prevented—though every day and
> hour shows us that they are the most natural and inevita-
> ble. I suppose that Time will do his usual work—Death
> has done his.[28]

To Sir Walter Scott he wrote:

> I have just lost my natural daughter, Allegra, by a fever.
> The only consolation, save time, is the reflection that she
> is either at rest or happy; for her few years (only five)
> prevented her from having incurred any sin except what
> we inherit from Adam.
> "Whom the gods love die young."[29]

And to Lord Holland, Byron confessed that "[Allegra's] death
. . . chilled my blood with horror. It was perhaps the most lively
sorrow I have ever felt."[30]

From Casa Magni, his new house at San Terenzo near Lerici,
Shelley wrote to Byron on May 3: "I have been compelled by
circumstances to tell Clare the real state of the case. I will not
describe her grief to you; you have already suffered too much;
and, indeed, the only object of this letter is to convey her last
requests to you."[31] Her wishes were to see the coffin before it
was sent to England (Shelley later dissuaded her from so doing)
and that Byron send her a miniature of Allegra and a lock of
her hair. These requests Byron granted.

That Byron's grief at his daughter's death was genuine is
incontestable. But of his overall feelings and behavior towards
her it is more difficult to make a judgment. Modern biographers
correctly see his feelings as mixed. Leslie Marchand, for ex-

ample, asserts that at times Byron regarded Allegra as an "extension of his ego," admiring as he did her beauty and cleverness and flattered by the attentions others gave her. At the same time "he was repelled when her temperament and her temper reflected his own less agreeable characteristics."[32] Iris Origo observes in Byron's correspondence "a complete masculine unawareness of a small child's character or needs—but not deliberate neglect, still less indifference." She adds that among Byron's mixed feelings towards Allegra, "bravado, affection, impatience, guilt," there existed also some "unjust, but not wholly unnatural" resentment on behalf of his legitimate daughter Ada whom he was not permitted to see.[33] Byron's love for Allegra was altogether in character: always self-centered, he loved her according to his fashion.

HARROW

Byron attended Harrow School from April 1800 through July 1805. Dr. Joseph Drury, the Headmaster, took particular care of him. Divining Byron's sensitivity about being put into a form with boys younger than himself, Drury arranged for private tutoring until the young lord could join classmates his own age. Dr. Drury also placed him in the house of his son, Henry, one of the assistant masters. After two years Byron had a falling out with Henry Drury and was placed with Mr. Benjamin Evans, but Dr. Drury managed to patch things up between Byron and his son, and the two eventually became lifelong friends. Byron's academic career at Harrow was not especially distinguished, although he did show some talent for oratory. But his most remembered role at Harrow came towards the very end of his stay and concerned the change of headmasters. The admired Dr. Drury announced his retirement in mid-March of 1805, and Byron—then seventeen—was drawn into the faction which supported Drury's brother Mark for the position. When Dr. George Butler, a Cambridge fellow, finally received the appointment (Archbishop Manners-Sutton of Canterbury had to break a tie vote of the School Governors between Butler and Mark Drury),

1. Byron, 1816

2. "The Separation, a Sketch from the private life of Lord IRON"

3. Claire Clairmont

4. Allegra

Caro il mio Pappa

Essendo tempo di Fiera
desidererei tanto una Visita
del mio Pappa, che hò molte voglie da levarmi, non
vorrà compiacere la sua
Allegrina che l'ho ama tanto?

5. Allegra's letter to her father, September, 1821

6. Shelley

7. John Murray's drawing room, 50 Albemarle Street, c.1815

8. John Murray II

Byron led an unsuccessful student rebellion against the new headmaster. In a poem written July of that year Byron said of Butler:

> Of narrow brain, yet of narrower soul,
> Pomposus holds you in his harsh control;
> Pomposus, by no social virtue sway'd,
> With florid jargon, and with vain parade;
> With noisy nonsense, and new-fangled rules,
> (Such as were ne'er before enforc'd in schools.)
> Mistaking *pedantry* for *learning's* laws,
> He governs, sanction'd but by self-applause;*
>
> ("On a Change of Masters at a Great Public School")

Like so many boys at English public schools, Byron found his first years at Harrow disagreeable. That this was so derived in part from the very nature of the system which sanctioned fagging and condoned bullying. Then too, Byron suffered from the clubfoot which provoked cruel humor until, with years, he was able to gain a certain ascendancy at the School. In later life Byron wrote, "I always hated *Harrow* till the last year and a half, but then I liked it."[1] In fact, from the moment Byron left school, Harrow became idealized in his memory and imagination. His removal from Harrow signaled the end of his romanticized boyhood and the interruption of the intense and passionate friendships that he had developed for young boys.** And it is only natural that these feelings for Harrow and its associations are prominent in the poetry of this period:

> Spot of my youth! whose hoary branches sigh,
> Swept by the breeze that fans thy cloudless sky;

* In "Childish Recollections" Pomposus-Butler is reviled as "the young usurper" (Butler was thirty-one at the time) whose "virtues are but known to few." Byron was later reconciled to Butler and regretted the lines which, had he published a new edition of *Hours of Idleness*, would have been changed to: "If once my muse a harsher portrait drew,/Warm with her wrongs, and deem'd the likeness true,/By cooler judgment taught, her fault she owns,—/With noble minds a fault confess'd, atones."

** The strongest such affection was for Lord Clare. In 1821, while journeying from Ravenna to Pisa to join Shelley, Byron met Clare on the road between Imola and Bologna: "This meeting annihilated for a moment all the years between the present time and the days of *Harrow*. It was a new and inexplicable feeling, like rising from the grave, to me."[2]

Where now alone I muse, who oft have trod
With those I lov'd thy soft and verdant sod.
("Lines Written Beneath An Elm in
the Churchyard of Harrow")

And again:

Seat of my youth! thy distant spire
 Recalls each scene of joy;
My bosom glows with former fire,—
 In mind again a boy.

. . . .

Each dear associate seems to say,
 'Friendship is Love without his wings!'
("L'Amitié est L'Amour sans
Ailes")

Accompanying such allusions to Harrow and its friendships was
a sentimental and romantic desire to be buried beneath the elm
in Harrow churchyard:

Here might I sleep where all my hopes arose,
Scene of my youth and couch of my repose;
For ever stretch'd beneath this mantling shade,
Press'd by the turf where once my childhood play'd;
Wrapt by the soil that veils the spot I loved,
Mix'd with the earth o'er which my footsteps moved.
("Lines Written Beneath . . .")

These and other poems that could be cited are youthful efforts, but Byron's attachment to Harrow was long-lived. As his
letters and journals indicate, mention of Harrow aroused in
him a kind of melancholic nostalgia, and Byron more than once
mentioned his wish to be buried there. Hence it comes as no
surprise that he directed his publisher, John Murray, to arrange
for Allegra's burial at Harrow. "You will regret to hear [he
wrote to Murray] that I have received intelligence of the death
of my daughter Allegra of a fever in the Convent of Bagna
Cavallo. . . . It is my present intention to send her remains to
England for sepulture in Harrow Church (where I once hoped
to have laid my own). . . . I wish the funeral to be very private."[3]
On May 26 he sent detailed instructions:

I wish [the body] to be buried in Harrow Church: there
is a spot in the Churchyard, near the footpath, on the
brow of the hill looking towards Windsor, and a tomb
under a large tree (bearing the name of Peachie, or
Peachey), where I used to sit for hours and hours when a
boy: this was my favourite spot; but, as I wish to erect
a tablet to her memory, the body had better be deposited
in the Church. Near the door, on the left hand as you
enter, there is a monument with a tablet containing these
words:—

"When Sorrow weeps o'er Virtue's sacred dust,
Our tears become us, and our Grief is just:
Such were the tears she shed, who grateful pays
This last sad tribute of her love and praise."

I recollect them (after seventeen years), not from any
thing remarkable in them, but because from my seat in
the Gallery I had generally my eyes turned towards that
monument: as near it as convenient I could wish Allegra
to be buried, and on the wall a marble tablet placed,
with these words:—

In memory of
Allegra,
daughter of G. G. Lord Byron,
who died at Bagnacavallo,
in Italy, April 20th, 1822,
aged five years and three months.
"I shall go to her,
but she shall not return to me."
2d Samuel, xii. 23.

The funeral I wish to be as private as is consistent with
decency; and I could hope that Henry Drury will, perhaps,
read the service over her.[4]

Murray sent the body of Allegra, which arrived in mid-Au-
gust, to B. Palmer & Son, Undertakers, 175 Piccadilly, and
through Harry Drury made inquiries about burial to the Vicar
of Harrow. The Reverend Joseph William Cunningham had
been ordained in 1802 and had served as curate at Ripley and
then at Clapham under the well-known John Venn, light of the
so-called Clapham sect. It was at Clapham that Cunningham

imbibed much of his staunch evangelicalism before coming to
Harrow as Vicar of St. Mary's in 1811. As Vicar, Cunningham
had close ties with the School. He preached before the boys
every Sunday (the School had not then its own chapel); he was
named one of the School Governors in 1818. Cunningham also
wrote various books of sermons and religious tracts and one
volume of poetry, but his most successful book by far—ten
editions in two years—was *The Velvet Cushion*, published in
1814. This small work contained the "autobiography" of a pulpit cushion and as such chronicled the changes of religious practice within the Church of England from the Reformation on-
wards. The book, which was staunchly evangelical and very
intolerant of both dissent and Catholicism,* earned Cunningham great popularity among the Low-Church party and the
predictable nickname, "Velvet Cunningham," from his enemies.

Cunningham's first communication with Murray begins po-
litely enough but immediately descends to the kind of unctuous
self-righteous cant that always invited disdain from those who
opposed him:

> Sir, Mr. Henry Drury was so good as to communicate to
> me a request conveyed to you by Lord Byron respecting
> the burial of a child in this church. Mr. H. Drury will
> probably have also stated to you my willingness to comply
> with the wish of Lord Byron. Will you forgive me, however,
> for so far trespassing upon you (though a stranger) as to
> suggest an inquiry whether it might not be practicable
> and desirable to fulfil for the *present* only a *part* of his
> lordship's wish—by burying the child, and putting up
> a tablet with simply its name upon the tablet; and thus
> leaving Lord B. more leisure to reflect upon the character
> of the inscription he may wish to be added. It does seem
> to me that whatever he may wish in the moment of his
> distress about the loss of this child, he will afterwards
> regret that he should have taken pains to proclaim to the
> world what he will not, I am sure, consider as honourable

* Some reviewers found the book so narrow-minded and prejudiced that
they accused Cunningham of satirically attacking the Church of England.
Cunningham wrote a clarification of his position in a preface that appeared in all later editions.

to his name. And if this be probable, then it appears to me the office of a true friend not to suffer him to commit himself but to allow his mind an opportunity of calm deliberation. I feel constrained to say that the inscription he proposed will be felt by every man of refined taste, to say nothing of sound morals, to be an offence against taste and propriety. My correspondence with his Lordship has been so small that I can scarcely venture myself to urge these objections. You perhaps will feel no such scruple. I have seen no person who did not concur in the propriety of stating them. I would entreat, however, that should you think it right to introduce my name into any statement made to Lord Byron, you will not do it without assuring him of my unwillingness to oppose the smallest obstacle to his wishes, or give the slightest pain to his mind. The injury which, in my judgment, he is from day to day inflicting upon society is no justification for measures of retaliation and unkindness.

> Your obedient and faithful Servant,
> J. W. Cunningham[5]

The meeting, which Mrs. Trollope was to celebrate in her poem, took place before Cunningham's next letter to Murray, this one curt and definitive:

The Churchwardens have been urged to issue their pro-hibition by several leading and influential persons, laymen, in the parish. You are aware that as to *ex-parishioners* the consent of the churchwardens is no less necessary than my own; and that therefore the enclosed prohibition* is decisive as to the putting up of the monument. You will oblige me by making known to Lord Byron the precise circumstances of the case.[6]

The funeral of Allegra took place September 10. Harry Drury conducted the service and entered her name in the parish register. The exact spot of burial is unknown, but it was prob-

---

* The "prohibition," dated September 17, read: "Honoured Sir, I ob-ject on behalf of the parish to admit the tablet of Lord Byron's child into the church. James Winkley, *Churchwarden*."

ably beneath the floor of the church vestibule. To this day no tablet commemorates her name.

Byron's final words on Allegra's burial at Harrow are contained in a letter to Augusta:

> There has been . . . a stupid story in the papers about the funeral of my poor little natural baby—which I directed to be as private as possible, & they say that she was to be buried and epitaphed opposite Lady B's pew—now—firstly —God help me! I did not know Lady B. had ever been in Harrow Church* and should have thought it the very last place she would have chosen,—and 2. my *real* instructions are in a letter to Murray of last summer—and the simplest possible as well as the inscription. But it has been my lot through life to be *never pardoned and almost always misunderstood*— . . . The story of this Child's burial is the epitome or miniature of the Story of my life. My regard for her—& my attachment for the spot where she is buried—made me wish that she should be buried *where*— though I never was *happy*—I was once less miserable as a boy—in thinking that I should be buried—and you see how they have distorted this as they do every thing into some story about Lady B.—of whom Heaven knows—I have thought much less than perhaps I should have done for these last four or five years.[7]

Byron wrote much the same message to Murray, but added a postscript on Cunningham:

> Why not tell me what were or are the objections to the inscription over poor little Allegra? Was there anything wrong in it?
> Cunningham is known for a notorious hypocrite—I remember Lady B telling me that she had heard of (from a Lady Olivia Sparrow—) or seen him—and that *her Lady B*'s belief was that he made his devotion subservient to his views of worldly advancement. He is the same

* In 1816, after the breakup of her marriage and after Byron's removal to the continent, Lady Byron met Cunningham; thereafter she frequented Harrow Church and occasionally stayed with the Cunningham family.

Coward who wrote to me that he did *not* intend some poem or other called *De Rancy** for a description of my character. I never cared whether he did or not; but some review had frightened him by hinting that he might as well have let me alone. I merely answered his letter (as I recollect at least) by a civil verbal message through Henry Drury. The best answer to all these liars and slaves will be my letter to you on the subject of the interment, which contains also the epitaph. You can add what is also true—from yourself—that I never was aware of Lady B's residing at Harrow or frequenting its church.[8]

MRS. TROLLOPE

The Trollope family resided at Harrow from 1816 to 1834, and during these years their fortunes were varied but on the whole disastrous. When Thomas Anthony Trollope removed his wife of seven years and their four children from Keppel Street, Russell Square, to a 400-acre Harrow farm leased from Lord Northwick, he did so with large hopes. His London law practice had been steadily diminishing, largely because of his impatient and disputatious attitude towards his colleagues and clients. But at Harrow he would, while keeping what was left of his law practice, regain his faltering health and try his hand at gentleman-farming. There was indeed little reason for believing he would succeed at farming, of which he knew nothing, after he showed signs of failing at law, in the practice of which he was considered quite competent. On the other hand, Thomas Anthony took cheer from the knowledge that he, or at least his eldest son, would one day inherit by entail a large and wealthy Hertfordshire estate called Julians. The present owner, his uncle Adolphus Meetkerke, was well over sixty and childless, and it was with a kind of grand impatience that Thomas Anthony named the large new house he built for himself at Harrow "Julians." But as his fourth son, Anthony, would write sixty years later: "That farm was the grave of all my father's hopes,

* Cunningham published *De Rancé* in 1815.

ambition, and prosperity, the cause of my mother's sufferings, and of those of her children, and perhaps the director of her destiny and of ours."[1] Scarcely had the Trollopes taken possession of their new house, when Uncle Meetkerke's wife died; thereupon—in a development worthy of one of Anthony's novels—the old man married a young woman who in short order presented him with a large family of his own. The quarrelsome nephew was disinherited. Thereafter Thomas Anthony's financial fortunes, health, and eventually even his sanity, declined until his unhappy end in 1835 as an indebted exile at Bruges.

Frances ("Fanny") Milton, daughter of the Reverend William Milton, Vicar of Heckfield, already had a reputation among her acquaintance for mischievous irreverence and satiric wit when she married Thomas Anthony Trollope in May of 1809. She was in nearly every respect the opposite of her husband. Where he was cold, dour, and pessimistic, she was warm, cheerful and sanguine; where he was serious and stern, she was fun-loving and easygoing. And, most importantly perhaps, whereas adversity could wear him down, it seemed only to strengthen her resiliency. In disaster she always landed on her feet. The disappointment over the Hertfordshire Julians did not prevent her from enjoying her own new Harrow Julians. Once established there, she made her drawing room the center of Harrow social life. Her circle included the Colonel Grants, her immediate neighbors; the numerous Drury family, who all but controlled Harrow School; Lady Milman, widow of the physician to Queen Charlotte; Dr. Pertz, a well-known German "savant"; the Merivale family; Guglielmo Pepe,* the Italian revolutionary; George Hayter, the painter;** Auguste Hervieu, a French painter; and Mary Russell Mitford, her long-time intimate friend. Cunningham the Vicar, although less welcome than he realized, often presented himself at Mrs. Trollope's entertainments.

But money was always a problem. While Fanny was entertain-

---

* At Pepe's suggestion, Mrs. Trollope in 1823 did an English verse translation of an ode by Alfieri in honor of Lafayette. Pepe had it published in the newspapers and sent copies to Lafayette.[2]

**Mr. Trollope sat for one of the lawyers in Hayter's most famous painting, "The Trial of Lord William Russell."

ing Harrow School masters, her sons were attending Harrow School only because local parishioners were admitted free of charge. (Both Trollope parents found embarrassing their sons' status as impoverished "day boarders," and when openings occurred at Winchester College, Mr. Trollope's own school, the boys were transferred, Thomas Adolphus in 1820, Henry in 1823, and Anthony in 1827.) Moreover, as the decade of the 1820's progressed, it became increasingly evident that the farm would never pay its way, and by 1827 the Trollopes were forced to lease Julians and remove to a smaller but still very commodious adjacent farmhouse, "Julians Hill" (the original for "Orley Farm" in Anthony's novel by that name). But still more drastic measures seemed called for, and in that same year the Trollopes determined to build a bazaar in the frontier town of Cincinnati: they would sell imported novelties to the natives. The preposterous plan called for Mrs. Trollope and her second son, Henry, together with her two young daughters, to go first to America to lay the groundwork. Much of the inspiration for this scheme had been Fanny's friend, Miss Frances Wright, a visionary reformer, feminist, lover of America, and quasi ward of the great Lafayette himself.* Mrs. Trollope's stay in America with all its frustrations and disillusionments is well-known; after three and one half years she returned home penniless, leaving behind at Cincinnati a grotesque and large "Graeco-Moresco-Gothic-Chinese-looking building"[3] ("Trollope's folly" the natives called it). The misadventure had exhausted the family's small resources. And when she arrived at Harrow, home was no longer Julians Hill but a tumbledown, decrepit farm at Harrow Weald to which Mr. Trollope had retired under further financial press. He had retreated into gloom, having for all practical purposes become an invalid, lacing himself with overly generous doses of calomel for his headaches. What energy remained to him was given exclusively toward his last ill-starred and poorly conceived project, the writing of an *Encyclopaedia Ecclesiastica*.** The only hope for the sinking household lay in the book

* Through Frances Wright the Trollopes had been introduced to Lafayette in 1824 and invited for a lengthy visit to La Grange. Fanny Trollope had all her life a knack for "collecting" famous people.
** One volume of the project was published over John Murray's imprint

Mrs. Trollope was fashioning from voluminous notes she had
taken in America.

Frances Trollope arrived home August 5, 1831, and by the
end of the month she had completed her manuscript. Mary
Russell Mitford gave her a letter of introduction to a publisher,
Whittaker, who sent the manuscript to a reader, Captain Basil
Hall, himself the author of a book very critical of the United
States (*Travels in North America, in the Years 1827 and 1828,
1829*). Captain Hall's approbation was enthusiastic: he person-
ally conveyed to Mrs. Trollope his support and guided her
through the signing of the contract with Whittaker. Preliminary
copies of the book were sent to the reviews, and Fanny had
good news even before publication: she wrote to her son
Thomas Adolphus that Lockhart of the *Quarterly* called it "the
cleverest woman's book he had read for a long time."[4] Another
of her letters describes the comical incident of her husband's
interview with John Murray about an advertisement of the
Encyclopaedia Ecclesiastica:

> *Murray*. . . . "By the bye!—*Trollope*—who the devil *is*
> Mrs. Trollope? Her book is the cleverest thing I ever read.
> I have read it through. So spirited!"
> *Trollope*. "The lady is my wife."
> *Murray*. "Why did she not bring it to me? It will sell like
> wildfire! She ought to have brought it to me. But I will
> help it all I can. You must introduce me to her."*

Mrs. Trollope continues:

---

in 1834. The full title page reads: "An Encyclopaedia Ecclesiastica; or, a
complete history of the Church, containing a full and compendious explanation of all ecclesiastical rites and ceremonies; a distinct and accurate
account of all denominations of Christians, from the earliest ages of Christianity to the present time; together with a definition of terms usually
occurring in ecclesiastical writers. By Thomas Anthony Trollope, LL.B.,
late Fellow of New College, Oxford, Barrister-at-Law."

* Mrs. Trollope met John Murray a few days later in the famous "back
room": "Such books! He showed me many MSS. of Lord Byron's: some
queer and curious enough. Your father was talking to him all the time
about his work, or I should have got more conversation with him. He
seemed very well inclined that way."[5] In 1834 John Murray published one
of Mrs. Trollope's books, *Belgium and Western Germany in 1833*.

There, my son, what do you think of that? May I not say like Lord Byron, "I awoke one morning and found myself famous"?[6]

Domestic Manners of the Americans was published on March 19, 1832, and Mrs. Trollope was famous at fifty-two. The book could not have been more auspiciously timed, coming as it did at the height of the intense debate over the Reform Bill. Her top-to-bottom criticism of the great democratic experiment across the Atlantic could not fail to delight conservatives at home. As her eldest son wrote: "It was emphatically the book of the season, was talked of everywhere, and read by all sorts and conditions of men and women. It was highly praised by all the Conservative organs of the press, and vehemently abused by all those of the opposite party."[7] The conservative *Quarterly*, which was owned by Murray, devoted forty pages to favorable comment and extensive excerpts: the reviewer describes Mrs. Trollope as "an English *lady* of sense and acuteness, who possesses very considerable power of expression"; the entire book is "clever and amusing" and the author is praised for her discussion of almost every aspect of American life. For example, the chapters on religion are warmly recommended for "those in any way distrustful of the benefits of the established church"; especially effective is her "lively description" of a prayer meeting, wherein she exposes it as an "extraordinary exhibition of hypocrisy, folly, fanatacism . . . and gross licentiousness." The notice closes with the observation that "almost every English liberal . . . who has recently travelled to the United States appears to have come back a convert to the old-fashioned doctrine of Toryism."[8]* On the other hand, the Whig *Edinburgh Review* roundly condemned *Domestic Manners* as a "spiteful, ill-considered and mischief making book"; the reviewer shrewdly observes that while Mrs. Trollope makes no mention of the personal objective of her mission to the United States "her whole book is engrained with the bitterness of its disappoint-

---

* See Mrs. Trollope's own admission: "I had a little leaning towards sedition myself when I set out [to visit the United States], but before I had half completed my tour I was quite cured." *Domestic Manners of the Americans* (Chap. v).

ment." One crucial criticism charges her with drawing "an indictment against a whole nation" from limited observations; another takes her to task for inconsistency born of a sense of social superiority: "She charges the Americans, as a nation, with want of religion, want of morals, and want of honesty. Nevertheless, want of refinement is the great fault!" And again there is the topical observation: "Returned to Harrow, her preface of March 1832 is an express advertisement against the Reform Bill. Four-and-thirty chapters of American scandal are dished up with the immediate purpose of contrasting the graceful virtue of a boroughmonger with the profligate vulgarity of a ten pound franchise."9

Her book went through four London editions in 1832 and as many in America. Mrs. Trollope was lionized:

> The Countess of Morley told me that she was certain that if I drove through London proclaiming who I was, I should have the horse taken off and be drawn in triumph from one end of the town to the other! The Honourable Mr. Somebody declared that my thunderstorm was the finest thing in prose or verse. Lady Charlotte Lindsay *implored* me to go on writing—never was anything so delightful. Lady Louisa Stewart told me that I had quite put English out of fashion and that everyone was talking Yankee talk.10

More important to Fanny Trollope than the notoriety was the money which the book brought in, nearly £1,000 in 1832. Characteristically, she spent rather easily; by September the family was back at Julians Hill, now newly furnished. She revived her "At Homes" in the drawing room. But she had become the bread-winner and had to continue writing to support her large family: a novel, *The Refugee in America*, appeared in 1833, followed by two more works, but again money was, as she said, "oozing fast." Moreover, it was discovered that Mrs. Trollope's lawyer-husband had through mistakes and omissions jeopardized both her marriage settlement money and the title to their London property. By April 1834 the situation became so desperate that Anthony was summoned to drive his bewildered father to the London docks whence he was spirited away to the Continent to avoid arrest for debt. In his *Autobiography* Anthony relates how on his return from London he found sheriff's officers in possession of Julians Hill and his sisters at work smuggling some books, china, and household silver out to their friends, the Grants, under whose roof the family was to huddle for a few days before embarking for Belgium.

The family settled at Bruges. It was here in a spacious but gloomy house called Château d'Hondt that Mrs. Trollope performed the most extraordinary of her many remarkable feats. Consumption, the family scourge,* had taken fast hold on her second son, Henry, and threatened her youngest daughter, Emily. Moreover, Mr. Trollope, although still working fitfully on his *Encyclopaedia Ecclesiastica,* was unmistakably failing. (He was sixty-one at the time, but a physician stated he would have put Thomas Anthony's age at more than eighty.)[11] Anthony described the household:

> my mother's most visible occupation was that of nursing. There were two sick men in the house, and hers were the hands that tended them. The novels went on, of course. . . . The doctor's vials and the ink-bottle held equal places in my mother's rooms. I have written many novels under many circumstances; but I doubt much whether I could write one when my whole heart was by the bedside of a dying son. Her power of dividing herself into two parts, and keeping her intellect by itself clear from the troubles of the world, and fit for the duty it had to do, I never saw equalled. . . . My mother went through [writing novels with a troubled spirit] unscathed in strength, though she performed all the work of day-nurse and night-nurse to a sick household;—for there were soon three of them dying.[12]

The three deaths came within fifteen months: at Bruges, Henry died in December, 1834, and Mr. Trollope in October, 1835; at

* Her third son, Arthur, had died of consumption at eleven in 1824; Cecilia Trollope, the last born, was to die of the same disease at thirty-two in 1849.

Hadley, Emily Trollope died in her seventeenth year in February, 1836. It was Frances Trollope's endurance through these two years of domestic tragedy while she was simultaneously earning the family food by turning out popular fiction that gained for her the epithet "indomitable."

In 1822, however, at the time of her poem on the burial of Allegra Byron, all these trials—the American business fiasco, the bankruptcy and flight, the triple deaths—were of course unforeseeable. Fanny was at the crest of her early Harrow prosperity. Finances were difficult, but not at a critical stage. Her eldest son, at least, had been sent to Winchester and was no longer a "day boarder" at Harrow School. Young Anthony had not yet entered upon his dismal scholastic career. Meanwhile her handsome drawing room at Julians provided Harrow with parties, *conversationi*, and "At Home" dramatic presentations in both French and English.

Thomas Adolphus Trollope in his autobiography noted that in the small-town atmosphere "*the* leading feature . . . of the social life of Harrow in those days consisted in a certain antagonism between the vicar, the Rev. Mr. Cunningham, and the clerical element of the school world, or perhaps it would be more correct to say the Drury element."[13] The Drurys included Mark Drury, second master, who, as we have seen, had come so very close to being named Headmaster in 1805. It was Mark Drury who offered free tuition to the Trollopes' eldest son in 1818. Because of his extreme obesity he had long ceased "going up," i.e. ascending the hill to the school proper, but conducted all his teaching at his boarding house. Mark's son, William, was fifth master in 1822; later he kept a school at Brussels where Anthony served briefly and unsuccessfully as classical usher in the summer of 1834.

But the unquestioned leader of the Drury faction and most important Harrow master of his day was "Old Harry" Drury. Appointed an assistant master in 1801 by his father, Headmaster Joseph Drury, his boarding house (originally called "The Abbey" but later "Druries") became the largest of the school. Harry was outspoken, bearish, and very learned: he was rumored to have all of Virgil and Horace by heart. And of course, as Byron's former tutor and continuing friend, he was Harrow's one genuine contact with Europe's most famous man of letters. Dean Merivale, who was a pupil at Harrow School from 1818 through 1824—the very years the Trollope boys attended—described Harry:

> he had the art of keeping his boys constantly in terror of his vigilance, and of managing a whole class while his attention was necessarily fixed upon only one at a time. . . . Upon all these numbers he actually impressed the conviction that he had his eye upon them one and all, and accurately gauged their acquirements and abilities. A big, stalwart man he was, genial but terrible; no other man has ever so elated, no other has ever so dismayed and confounded me. The success which attended his tuition was remarkable, and his pupils almost uniformly took the lead in the competitions for prizes and scholarships. His supremacy in this respect was generously admitted by the headmaster and by all his associates, while his force of character and promptness in action gave him high authority in the general government of the institution.[14]

Thomas Adolphus Trollope contrasted Harry Drury and Cunningham, rivals for influence at Harrow:

> Harry Drury . . . was a man of decidedly literary tastes, though they shared his devotion with those of a *bon vivant*. He was a ripe scholar, and undoubtedly the vicar's superior in talent and intellect. But he was essentially a coarse man, coarse in manner and coarse in feeling. Cunningham was the reverse of all this. He was, I believe, the son of a London hatter, but in external manner and appearance he was a more gentlemanlike man than any of the Harrow masters of that day, save Dr. Butler. He had the advantage, too, of a handsome person and good presence. But there was a something *too* suave and *too* soft, carrying with it a certain suspicion of insincerity which prevented him from presenting a genuine specimen of the real article. I believe his father purchased the living for him under circumstances which were not altogether

free from suspicion of simony.* . . . There was . . . a story of his having, soon after coming to Harrow . . . attributed with much self-complacency his presentation to the living to his having upon some occasion preached before Lord Northwick!—a result which no Harrow inhabitant, clerk or layman, would have believed in the case of his lordship . . . if the preacher had been St. Paul. But . . . *Audi alteram partem*![15]

One incident, doubtless typical, serves to illustrate the Drury-Cunningham tension: Mark Drury's two "remarkably pretty" and "thoroughly good" daughters, seated in the pew immediately in front of Cunningham's pulpit, apparently talked or laughed during the sermon, whereupon Cunningham stopped his discourse, leaned over the pulpit cushion, and said aloud that he would resume his sermon "when his hearers could listen to it with decency!" For a long time thereafter, Harry Drury never "came within speaking distance of the vicar without growling 'Brawler!' in a perfectly audible voice."[16]

Mrs. Trollope's relationship with the Vicar was, outwardly at least, a bit more cordial; we know that Cunningham frequented her "At Homes." But she was very much of the Drury faction and never lost an opportunity to have a little fun at Cunningham's expense. For example, according to Thomas Adolphus, she told a pretty eighteen year old neighbor's daughter to beware lest Cunningham's kiss of peace "change its quality if repeated!"[17] Michael Sadleir recorded upon "the direct testimony of one of the Grant family" an example of the kind of anecdote Mrs. Trollope loved to retail: Cunningham one day asked her whether she thought the games of charades with which she entertained young people at parties were a "suitable diversion for young ladies":

> "Why not, Mr. Cunningham?" demanded [Mrs. Trollope]. "Mrs. Cunningham has evening parties to which we are always glad to go to hear your daughters play upon the piano."

* The *DNB* says that the presentation to Harrow "had been bought by Cunningham's father-in-law," Robert Williams of Moor Park, Surrey.

"Ah, yes," replied the Vicar "but my daughters always have their backs to the audience."[18]

And in 1826 in a letter to Thomas Adolphus Mrs. Trollope herself relates a little encounter with Cunningham:

We dined at Mr. B.'s last Tuesday, and alas! I was the only lady of the party not "pious." I was quite thrown out, when they began to talk of selling £200 worth of pincushions for various Christian purposes. Mr. Cunningham was there, and told me that he had heard that I had been amusing myself at his expense, by repeating what he had said about the *virtuous* manner in which certain young ladies played the piano-forte. I told him that I had; upon which he turned the other cheek and asked me "why?" Whereupon I answered with my usual sincerity, "because you deserved it, sir."[19]

It must surely have been an added humiliation for Mrs. Trollope when her husband, forced to vacate Julians, leased it to none other than Cunningham. But in spite of her antipathy to the Vicar, there had never been an open break. Indeed, upon Mrs. Trollope's return from America, we discover Cunningham taking upon himself the duty of presenting to her Dr. Longley, who had been appointed Headmaster of Harrow School during her absence. And again, when the Trollopes were dispossessed of Julians Hill and Mrs. Trollope and her children were sheltered for a few days with the Grants, Cunningham "paid a long visit to Mrs. Trollope, and invited her daughters to his house."[20]

The cause célèbre at Harrow over the burial of Allegra Byron had an irresistible attraction for Mrs. Trollope: there was the "singular vestry meeting" with not only the Vicar, but all the reverend masters of Harrow School ("except poor old Mark") and many "leading parishioners" present; there was the puritanical verdict; and finally there was the "innate and invincible flunkeyism" of Cunningham who had the temerity to ask Harry Drury to convey his admiration of *Cain* to Byron—and this two minutes after denying Byron's request for a commemorative tablet over his daughter's tomb. T. A. Trollope, who had our manuscript to hand while writing his autobiography,[21] tells how a copy of his mother's poem was shown to Harry Drury, who, "though he himself was not altogether spared, was so delighted with it that he rewarded it by the present of a very remarkable autograph of Lord Byron,"—a copy in Byron's hand of his poem, "Lines to a Lady Weeping."[22]

One can readily believe that Frances Trollope was delighted with the Byron autograph, for she was assuredly much subject to "Byromania." Her son Anthony says of her: "she raved also of him of whom all such ladies were raving then, and rejoiced in the popularity and wept over the persecution of Lord Byron."[23] Some of Mrs. Trollope's adoration for Byron crept into *Domestic Manners*, where she satirized a *"serious* gentleman," one "said to be a scholar and a man of reading," whom she met at Cincinnati:

> Our poor Lord Byron, as may be supposed, was the bull's eye against which every dart in his little black quiver was aimed. I had never heard any serious gentleman talk of Lord Byron at full length before, and I listened attentively. It was evident that the noble passages which are graven on the hearts of the genuine lovers of poetry had altogether escaped the serious gentleman's attention; and it was equally evident that he knew by rote all those that they wish the mighty master had never written. I told him so, and I shall not soon forget the look he gave me. (chap. ix)

It is not too much to suggest, as has one critic, that the inspiration for the strange architecture of the Cincinnati Bazaar itself "came from an imagination steeped in the Oriental fantasies of Lord Byron and Tom Moore."[24]

Frances Trollope's poem, "Lines written on the burial of the daughter of a celebrated author,"* is representative of a particular species of Byromania, namely the enormous literature in-

* Anthony's version of his mother's poem contains the words "by a celebrated authoress" in the title. In truth we are not certain of the original title.

spired by and imitative of *Don Juan*. Probably no poem in the language has had as many "continuations," some of which were presented as such by their authors, while others were passed off as "discovered" cantos, supposedly written by Byron. But even more numerous than these sequels were poems imitating the meter and style of Byron's masterpiece.[25] It had been in *Beppo* (1817) that Byron departed from the characteristic Popean couplets of *Childe Harold* and took up the Pulcian *ottava rima*. Byron's immediate inspiration for using *ottava rima* in mock-heroic style had been John Hookham Frere's *Prospectus and Specimen of an Intended National Work* ("by the Brothers Whistlecraft"), a poem drawn from Pulci's *Morgante Maggiore*.[26] The great advantages of the new form—particularly as rendered in *Don Juan* in what modern readers universally regard as Byron's best poetic voice—included flexibility and adaptability to colloquialisms and a "prose" manner. Especially useful was the two-line resolution, frequently changing the mood from serious to light or ironically recasting the first six lines of the stanza. Then too in this kind of mock heroic poetry Byron could exploit to excellent purpose something he was master of, the imperfect or outrageous rhyme.

Mrs. Trollope was no more in Byron's class than any of his other admirers and imitators; she was, as Anthony said, "a writer of prose, [who] revelled in satire."[27] The only published poetry from her pen was the slight volume called *The Mother's Manual, or Illustrations on Matrimonial Economy, An Essay in Verse* (1833). Some unpublished one-act verse dramas have also survived (see Appendix). Both the *Mother's Manual* and the dramas are in couplets, but for "Lines on the Burial" the *ottava rima*, mock-heroic *Don Juan*-style serves her well. The poem opens in John Murray's celebrated "back shop" where the famous publisher's advisors and literary hangers-on gather:

> In sweet exchange of thoughts legitimate
>   The well behaving synod sat most civil:
> One praised the bishop's charge, who had of late
>   So clearly proved that knowledge was the evil
> Would surest bring destruction on the state.

But the pious and patriotic talk is interrupted by the arrival of
a package which had caused some problem with the excisemen;
Murray settles the difficulty

> in accents douce and loyal,
> For taxes and excise are all but royal.

The package and accompanying letter enter at an unpropitious
moment, namely "in the presence of so many reverend folk,"
who wrest from Murray an admission of the contents of the
package:

> Send you a daughter Murray in a cask?
> What daughter? Is't a daughter of his brain?

Murray's friends coax from him the whole story:

> So forth they passed—each eager to reveal
> To his own chosen circle of dear friends,
> All they had promised Murray to conceal.

Thereafter we read what Anthony would call the "capital pictures" of the debaters at the Harrow churchwardens' meeting.
Some of Mrs. Trollope's master's wit and sprightliness can be
seen throughout, and two recognizable resemblances to *Don
Juan* come to mind at once: the comparison of the northern
and the southern European and the constant anti-cant stance.
Where Mrs. Trollope is weakest is on Byron himself; whenever
she becomes serious, she is flat and wrongheaded, and about her
idol she is all seriousness. She describes Byron in terms all but
superhuman: he is the "mighty bard," "the glory of the land";
his is an "awful mind" which no "earthly censor" must presume
to judge, his is a "mighty heart." Mrs. Trollope even descends
to cant: for if she can be excused for not knowing the par-
ticulars of Byron's treatment of Allegra (the details of which
were known to only Claire, Shelley, and a few trusted corre-
spondents), one can still wish she had not attempted to let her
worshipful imagination fill in the gaps in her knowledge. She
pictures Allegra clinging "round [Byron's] soul" for "five summers," after which

He saw her sicken and he watched her die,
  The soft small hands' last pressure was his own.
His the last glance of meaning from her eye,
  And his to clasp her when the spark was flown.

Knowing what we do of the case, we find the lines incongruous today. Anthony Trollope's closing note to his mother's poem well says: "this is an eccentric idea—this setting up Byron as the champion of virtue—but admiration does wonders. There is much wit in the lampoon, and it is interesting to me from a variety of causes."

ANTHONY TROLLOPE

Before looking into the most remarkable aspect of the entire Salmagundi manuscript, Trollope's notes, it will be well to recount briefly Anthony's miserable childhood and youth. Trollope never deliberately revealed much of his personal life in his novels or even in his letters. As for his *Autobiography*, he insists in the very first sentence that "it will not be so much my intention to speak of the little details of my private life, as of what I . . . have done in literature." And by and large Trollope stayed to his resolve: for example, of his marriage to Rose Heseltine in 1844 we are told only that it was "like the marriage of other people, and of no special interest to any one except my wife and me."[1] But if his reticence about his personal life is relentless throughout most of the book, in the first three chapters Trollope has given us a very revealing and affecting view of his early life.

Anthony entered Harrow School in 1822, an impoverished day-boarder among the children of aristocrats and the well-to-do: he describes his "ignominy":

I was only seven. . . . I was never spared; and was not even allowed to run to and fro between our house and the school without a daily purgatory. No doubt my appearance was against me. I remember well, when I was still the junior boy in the school, Dr. Butler, the headmaster, stopping

me in the street, and asking me . . . whether it was possible
that Harrow School was disgraced by so disreputably dirty
a little boy as I! Oh, what I felt at that moment! But I
could not look my feelings. I do not doubt that I was
dirty;—but I think that he was cruel. He must have known
me as he was wont to see me, for he was in the habit of
flogging me constantly. Perhaps he did not recognise me
by my face.[2]

After three ineffectual years at Harrow School, Anthony, still
the "lag" or "junior boy," was sent upon the advice of his tutor,
Henry Drury, to a private school at Sunbury kept by Arthur
Drury. Here, in addition to the usual embarrassments attendant
on his poverty, Anthony suffered through an entire term un-
justly accused of homosexual practice:

> I remember well how . . . four boys were selected as having
> been the perpetrators of some nameless horror. . . . I was
> one of the four, innocent as a babe, but adjudged to have
> been the guiltiest of the guilty. . . . It broke my heart,
> knowing myself to be innocent, and suffering also under
> the almost equally painful feeling that the other three—no
> doubt wicked boys—were the curled darlings of the school,
> who would never have selected me to share their wicked-
> ness. . . . All that was fifty years ago, and it burns me now
> as though it were yesterday.

Arthur Drury, it seems, had thought that Anthony, "having
come from a public school, might be supposed to be the leader
of wickedness!"[3]

At twelve, Anthony was transferred to Winchester College.
This was in 1827, and his mother, who was shortly to leave for
America, felt secure in placing Anthony under the care of his
older brother. Thomas Adolphus accepted the responsibility
seriously and took it upon himself to thrash Anthony daily with
a big stick. But when his "draconian" brother left Winchester to
accompany Mr. Trollope to Cincinnati, Anthony's plight grew
even worse:

> My college bills had not been paid, and the school trades-
> men who administered to the wants of the boys were told

not to extend their credit to me. Boots, waistcoats, and pocket-handkerchiefs . . . were closed luxuries to me. My schoolfellows of course knew that it was so, and I became a Pariah. It is the nature of boys to be cruel. I have sometimes doubted whether among each other they do usually suffer much, one from the other's cruelty; but I suffered horribly! I could make no stand against it. I had no friend to whom I could pour out my sorrows. I was big, and awkward, and ugly, and, I have no doubt, skulked about in a most unattractive manner. Of course I was ill-dressed and dirty. But, ah! how well I remember all the agonies of my young heart; how I considered whether I should always be alone; whether I could not find my way up to the top of that college tower, and from thence put an end to everything?[4]

After three years at Winchester, Anthony returned to Harrow. He lived alone with his gloomy and disillusioned father at the tumbledown farmhouse at Harrow Weald, whence he was once again sent as day-boarder to Harrow School, trudging the three miles between home and school four times daily:

Perhaps the eighteen months which I passed in this condition, walking to and fro on those miserable dirty lanes, was the worst period of my life. I was now over fifteen, and had come to an age at which I could appreciate at its full the misery of expulsion from all social intercourse. I had not only no friends, but was despised by all my companions. . . . What right had a wretched farmer's boy, reeking from a dunghill, to sit next to the sons of peers,— or much worse still, next to the sons of big tradesmen who had made their ten thousand a-year? The indignities I endured are not to be described. As I look back it seems to me that all hands were turned against me,—those of masters as well as boys.*[5]

* Sir William Gregory, who entered Harrow School in 1831, and who in later life became Trollope's friend, corroborated Anthony's story in his own autobiography: "I became intimate with Anthony Trollope, who sat next to me. He was a big boy, older than the rest of the form, and without exception the most slovenly and dirty boy I ever met. He was not only slovenly in person and in dress, but his work was equally dirty. His exer-

When Mrs. Trollope returned from America, published *Domestic Manners,* and moved her family back into Julians Hill, the circumstances of Anthony's schooling improved somewhat:

> The three miles became half a mile, and probably some salutary changes were made in my wardrobe. . . . But I was never able to overcome—or even to attempt to overcome—the absolute isolation of my school position. Of the cricket-ground, or racket-court, I was allowed to know nothing. And yet I longed for these things with an exceeding longing. I coveted popularity with a coveting which was almost mean.[7]

Trollope left Harrow School when he was nearly nineteen, having begun there at seven. He insists he learned almost nothing: "During the whole of those twelve years no attempt had been made to teach me anything but Latin and Greek, and very little attempt to teach me those languages." When Anthony left Harrow in 1834 he was a monitor and "seventh boy," a position he achieved by "gravitation upwards." He never got any of the numerous scholastic prizes so prodigally handed out. What he most remembered from all three schools was the beatings: "I feel convinced in my mind that I have been flogged oftener than any human being alive."[8]

We have already seen Trollope's part in his father's flight to Belgium to escape arrest for debt. Anthony described himself at Bruges as "an idle, desolate hanger-on, that most hopeless of

---

cises were a mass of blots and smudges. These peculiarities created a great prejudice against him, and the poor fellow was generally avoided. It is pitiable to read in his autobiography, just published, how bitter were his feelings at that time, and how he longed for the friendship and companionship of his comrades, but in vain. . . . I had plenty of opportunities of judging Anthony, and I am bound to say, though my heart smites me sorely for my unkindness, that I did not like him. I avoided him, for he was rude and uncouth, but I thought him an honest, brave fellow. He was no sneak. His faults were external; all the rest of him was right enough. But . . . poor Trollope was tabooed, and had not, so far as I am aware, a single friend. . . . He gave no sign of promise whatsoever, was always in the lowest part of the form, and was regarded by masters and by boys as an incorrigible dunce."[6]

human beings, a hobbledehoy of nineteen, without any idea of a career, a profession, or a trade."[9] Then, from some unexpected quarter came an offer to make Anthony a commissioned officer in an Austrian cavalry regiment. The plan called for Trollope to devote one year to acquiring the necessary knowledge of German and French; accordingly, he went to a school kept by William Drury at Brussels where, in exchange for the opportunity to learn these languages, he was to serve as a classical usher. But after Anthony had spent six unsuccessful weeks in this post, he was tendered a junior clerkship in the London General Post Office. The offer had been arranged through a friend of Mrs. Trollope, Mrs. Clayton Freeling, whose father-in-law was Secretary of the Post Office at Saint Martins-le-Grand.* Thus, by the autumn of 1834 Trollope entered upon his career as a civil servant,** having moved into lodgings (shared briefly with his brother) in Little Marlborough Street. It was at this address that he finished putting together his "Salmagundi," which he had begun in Brussels.

This manuscript, the full title of which is "Salmagundi— aliena, 1834" is from any point of view an oddity. (Whether or not Trollope derived his title from Washington Irving's *Salmagundi Papers* is unknown.) Trollope's "Salmagundi" included, in addition to the lengthy "Lines on the Burial," three short poems that exhibit curious interests. The first is a lampoon on the Regent and Marshal Blücher, gleaned from the *Morning Chronicle,* June, 1814; the second concerns a repentant and disillusioned Lady Caroline Lamb; the last is a kind of violently melancholic *carpe diem* love poem. All three are of unknown authorship. But whatever the authorship of these poems, the 32-page potpourri with Trollope's own footnotes is the earliest

* Samuel Smiles maintained that John Murray helped secure Anthony's position at the Post Office.[10]
** Trollope eventually rose to a high position in the Post Office and retired only in 1867. But his first years as clerk in the General Post Office in London were almost as unhappy as had been his Harrow years. Expected to live like a "London gentleman" on £90 a year, he was constantly in debt and hounded by creditors. He seems to have been careless and dissatisfied in his work, unproductive in his vague literary aspirations, discontented with his social life. Altogether he qualified as the black sheep of the family, in both their eyes and his own.

manuscript from the hand of the future chronicler of Barsetshire.

Perhaps the most salient impression one receives from the
"Salmagundi" is that Trollope at nineteen was very much pre-
occupied with literature. The very fact that Anthony as a
young man, either in his first position of responsibility at Brussels or truly independent and living on his own in London,
would painstakingly produce such a manuscript is remarkable.
On the other hand, his literary aspirations were understandable
enough: his was, after all, a "writing family"; his mother, who
always loved literary talk* and who during the 1820's dabbled
in amateur poetry and drama, had by now become one of England's best known woman writers; his father, who had published
in 1823 a short work called *A Treatise on the Mortgage of
Ships*, had brought out in 1834 the first (and only) volume of
his *Encyclopaedia Ecclesiastica*. Moreover, in October 1832 the
entire Trollope family, re-established at Julians Hill, started its
own manuscript journal, *The Magpie*, "a weekly Magazine of
Literature, Politics, Science, and Art" (as the title page ex-
plained), a venture aptly described as "a half-joking, half-seri-
ous playing at literature."[12] Although Henry Trollope, not Anthony, was editor, one need have no hesitation about accepting
the sometimes unreliable T.H.S. Escott's word that Anthony
"had the satisfaction of finding his little contributions in prose
and verse generally given a place."[13] Again, there is evidence
that Trollope's claim to have learned nothing but a little Latin
and Greek at Harrow may not be entirely accurate: Lord Bess-
borough, schoolmate of Trollope during the 1830's, remarked
of this passage from the *Autobiography*:

> Mr. Trollope must have forgotten the weekly English
> themes which the present writer, Lord Bessborough, had
> reason to remember, because, having taken extraordinary
> pains with one for which a small prize was to be given, he

* John Herman Merivale's Diary for February 11, 1822, tells of an
evening party at which the guests included the Italian poet Ugo Foscolo
and the Trollopes: "Mrs. Trollope came in her deepest blue stockings. . . .
the 'Siddonian glances' which Kean detected the other night in Mrs. Trollope were entirely thrown away on Foscolo, who shrugged up his shoulders
and observed that she was *very blue*."[11]

went anxiously to Dr. Longley for his decision, having, as
he believed, done fairly well. "You did well," replied the
head-master, "but, you see, Trollope writes better English
than you do, at present."[14]

Also noteworthy in this matter of Trollope's literary aspiration
is his earliest extant letter, dated 24 May 1835: after discussing
with publisher Richard Bentley a delay in the printing of
Mrs. Trollope's latest book, Anthony requests Bentley's assistance "in procuring the insertion of lucubrations of my own in
any of the numerous periodical magazines &c which come out
in such monthly swarms."[15] Finally, Trollope writes in his *Autobiography* that he kept a journal for ten years, or from about
1830 to 1840, the volumes of which remained in his possession
"unregarded—never looked at—till 1870, when I examined
them, and, with many blushes, destroyed them. They convicted
me of folly, ignorance, indiscretion, idleness, extravagance, and
conceit. But they had habituated me to the rapid use of pen and
ink, and taught me how to express myself with facility."[16] And
a few pages further on: "I had often told myself since I left
school that the only career in life within my reach was that of
an author, and the only mode of authorship open to me that of
a writer of novels. In the journal which I read and destroyed a
few years since, I found the matter argued out before I had
been in the Post Office two years."*[17] Perhaps in 1834 he was
still considering poetry or criticism.

Trollope's critical notes have a knowing ring; one would
think them the remarks of an old hand. He rightly observes
that the first poem of his collection is in Tom Moore's style.
On his mother's style he is severe, even captious: to the lines
"For a bel-esprit can have no possession/ Which helps him on
so much in his profession" (stanza 27), Trollope comments:
"What possession this means is not evident . . . perspicuity of
style is by no means one of the merits of this poem." To be sure,

* Trollope's fiction contains two partial self-portraits of himself during
his London clerkship days: Charley Tudor of *The Three Clerks* is an aspir-
ing author, and Johnny Eames of *The Small House at Allington* "was a
deep critic, often writing down his criticisms in a lengthy journal which
he kept. He could write quickly, and with understanding" (chap. xiv).

his own "corrections" are not always felicitous. When he insists on adding words to lines he usually disturbs the meter while achieving very little more clarity; thus his insistence that "Whilst those the loudest in thy chorus [*who*] sing" must have the relative to be intelligible is faulty (stanza 35; see also 36). One further example of his censorious attitude: to the perfectly clear lines "Seek not to all in power to appear/ Bound to their cause with such devotion deep," Trollope adds the bewildering footnote: "These lines are bad, 1st—because power is properly only one syllable. 2nd because—the words are twisted about so much, and as their refers to power, it should be in a separate division of the sentence—at least, wherever the fault lies—there is one somewhere, as it is very obscure" (stanza 47).

Trollope not only finds fault with his mother's poetic style, but he takes amused delight in remarking on her flip-flop politics. (Indeed Anthony's general attitude towards his mother seems condescending, if not mildly antipathetic. Commentators have not been lacking who have insisted that Anthony felt somewhat neglected by his mother. Thomas Adolphus was her eldest and favorite son; Henry was next both in favor and age; then too Henry, and Arthur—the third son, who died at eleven —lacked Anthony's robust health and undoubtedly received more maternal attention.) Trollope in his very first note, after interjecting "How some people's politics turn!" calls his mother "the staunchest of staunch tories." Were she writing now, the sentiments ridiculed in stanza three would be "all that was divine and inspired! Never mind! Southey wrote Wat Tyler." And in another note he writes: "the fair authoress mixes up Toryism and Cant in rather a singular and unjust manner—but she has learnt her errors by this time." Here we see Trollope's characteristic consistency underscored: forty years later in the *Autobiography* he would write of his mother:

> She had loved society, affecting a somewhat liberal *rôle*, and professing an emotional dislike to tyrants, which sprung from the wrongs of would-be regicides and the poverty of patriot exiles. An Italian marquis who had escaped with only a second shirt from the clutches of some archduke whom he had wished to exterminate, or a French

prolétaire with distant ideas of sacrificing himself to the cause of liberty, were always welcome to the modest hospitality of her house. In after years, when marquises of another caste had been gracious to her, she became a strong Tory, and thought that archduchesses were sweet. But, with her, politics were always an affair of the heart,— as, indeed, were all her convictions. Of reasoning from causes, I think that she knew nothing.*[18]

But Trollope's criticism is not all negative; his final note asserts: "There is much wit in the lampoon, and it is interesting to me from a variety of causes." One of his chief interests here was probably Byron. Trollope begins by dissociating himself from what he considers the "vast nonsense" in his mother's worshipful attitude: "his Lordship was certainly a clever man— but as selfish a bonvivant as ever lived and no more worthy of the etherial character so often given him than I am. I do not wish to break through that awful 'judge not'—but if I were in the habit of doing so—Lord B'ˢ case would be no sticking point." On the other hand, ample evidence survives to indicate that Byron was one of Trollope's favorite poets. In his *Autobiography*, Trollope, while discussing how he obtained his clerkship in the Post Office without benefit of competitive civil service examination, lists his modest accomplishments as of 1834: "I had read Shakespeare and Byron and Scott, and could talk about them."[20] And of the autobiographical young Johnny Eames of *The Small House at Allington* Trollope remarks: "he could read and understand Shakespeare. He knew much,—by far too much,—of Byron's poetry by heart" (chap. xiv). In 1855 Trollope included Byron (alone among the great Romantic poets save for Burns) in his list of eighteen "giants" of English literature.[21] Byron also figured prominently among the poets whom Trollope read aloud during the last years of his life.[22]

* This passage drew a strong rejoinder from Thomas Adolphus: "Now there is hardly a word of this in which Anthony is not more or less mistaken . . . simply because he had not adequate opportunities for close observation. . . . I think that I knew her as few sons know their mothers."[19] But it is precisely because Thomas Adolphus was so close to his subject that we today tend to accept Anthony's analysis. It is, after all, not a terribly harsh one.

Finally, Trollope's interest in his mother's satire was enhanced by a personal acquaintance with the Harrow participants. Of Dr. Butler, for example, Trollope says, "tho' he was very severe to little boys, he was a very inefficient master—and the school went on declining till he resigned—he was altogether unable to keep the head boys in order, and rather feared them, than was feared by them." Trollope seems not to have thought very highly of the Drurys—"prize clergymen" he calls them— except perhaps for "old Harry," the one principal at the vestry meeting for whom Mrs. Trollope had a good word. Anthony calls her complimentary lines "not bad" and asserts that Drury's "frankness is bearishness—but he is a good natured fellow— though he has often nearly plagued my life out." Similarly the lines on Benjamin Evans, third master, are called "good—particularly as much severer satire was well deserved by this little fellow, from the point from whence these lines came—and was not omitted from want of ability." In short, Trollope preferred the latter part or Harrow section of the poem which he called "very clever, true and well put."

Two of Trollope's notes on the Harrow participants will serve to give us examples of his earliest prose style. Of his mother's remarks on William Mills, sixth master, Trollope writes:

> This is a capital picture of Mills. I used always to stick
> up for Mills—I don't know why—for he is a weak, quarrel
> some, conceited ass—not to speak of his absolute vulgarity
> and ignorance. He has always a most laughable mode of
> keeping up his dignity, and walks with his nose ludicrously
> in the air. He had the upper shell when I was in that
> part—he used constantly to make bad puns on the boys'
> names. When Evans died old Harry was made under
> master but still kept the 5th form instead of taking the
> third as usual, as Mills was too much of an ass.

And of Cunningham:

> he may well be called "mild eyed"—a man almost wor
> shipped by the low church at Harrow, very unpopular with

the gentry, and much feared by the poor—a most despicable hypocrite—a gentleman like man with very
pleasing manners and a sweet voice. I used to talk to
Cunningham a good deal at one time, and recall he always
used to be very civil to me, but he is a cringing hypocrite
and a most confounded liar, and would give his eyes to
be a bishop. . . .

The manner is somewhat harsh and brash, yet Trollope at
nineteen could write. But the gentle, tolerant, ironic humor of
Barsetshire was still twenty years away.

AFTERWARDS

Byron survived Allegra by only two years. After her death he
felt all the more painfully his powerlessness to see his legitimate
daughter Ada, and a few months before his own end at Missolonghi Byron "adopted" a little Turkish girl of nine named
Hatadje. The girl and her mother, whose entire family had
been killed in the Turkish-Greek struggles, were staying at the
home of Julius Millingen, an English doctor. According to
Millingen's account:

> [Byron] became so struck by Hatajè's beauty, the naïveté
> of her answers, and the spiritedness of her observations
> on the murderers of her brethren, that he decided on
> adopting her. "Banish fear for ever from your mind,"
> said he to the mother; "your child shall, henceforth, be
> mine. I have a daughter in England. To her I will send
> you. They are both of the same age; and as she is alone,
> she will, no doubt, like a companion who may, at times,
> talk to her of her father. . . ." He immediately ordered
> more costly dresses to be made for them, than those I
> had given them; and sent to Hatajè a necklace of sequins.
> Twice a week, I was desired to send them to his house.
> He would then take the little girl on his knees, and caress
> her with all the fondness of a father.[1]

The preposterous idea of sending to Ada and his estranged wife this adopted Moslem "daughter" would never have succeeded, even had Byron not met his premature death at Missolonghi on April 19, 1824.

Word of Byron's death did not reach England and John Cam Hobhouse, his executor, until May 14, and the body did not arrive until July 2. Henry Drury tried unsuccessfully to persuade Hobhouse to have the burial in Harrow Church,* and the remains were eventually interred in the family vault of Hucknall Torkard Church near Newstead.

Two weeks after Allegra's death, Shelley, her persistent advocate in life, saw her in a "vision." The incident is recorded in the diary of Edward Williams, with whom Shelley had been walking on the ocean terrace at Casa Magni:

> [Shelley] grasped me violently by the arm, and stared steadfastly on the white surf that broke upon the beach under our feet. Observing him sensibly affected, I demanded of him if he were in pain; but he only answered by saying "There it is again! there!" He recovered after some time, and declared that he saw, as plainly as he then saw me, a naked child (Allegra, who had recently died) rise from the sea, clasp its hands as if in joy, and smiling at him.[2]

A month later Shelley drowned in the Mediterranean off Viareggio.

Mary Shelley took lodgings at Harrow from 1832 through 1836 while Percy Florence Shelley attended Harrow School. Mary found Harrow a "dull inhospitable place," but of the School she wrote: "the more I see the more I like. . . . The boys here have liberty to the verge of license—yet of the latter, save the breaking of a few windows now and then, there is none."**[3]

---

* Through Hobhouse's cooperation, Drury did have the minor satisfaction of adopting two of Byron's dogs.

** In the same year in which Mary Shelley wrote these lines (1834), Byron's widow gave her impression of Harrow School: a "nursery" of "corruption and crime"; "The elder boys resort habitually to the Red

9. Frances Trollope

10. Harrow School Room, 1816

11. The Churchyard at Harrow: Byron and the Peachey stone

12. Rev. Henry Drury

13. Rev. Joseph William Cunningham

14. Orley Farm (Julians Hill)

40

He stood apart nor owned the Goddess' power
Yet sometime he would listen to her too.
And I have heard that in an evil hour
He has been known to laud the pensioned crew,
And speak with great respect of all in power,
And say that mischief lurked in what was new,
But yet I much believe some latent joke
Lay shrouded in the ultra words he spoke.

41

Before him stood looking most wondrous wise
The worthy little Evans of the vale.
His was no start of makebelieve surprise
When as he listened to the wondrous tale,
He opened wide his horror stricken eyes,
And blessed his stars that he was not so frail.
For he was sure not all the world could say
He'd quitted Mrs Evans night or day.

The fair authoress mixes up Toryism & Cant in rather
a singular & unjust manner — but she has learnt
her error by this time — Old Harry has
as little cant as any man I know — but he is apt
to praise the pensioned crew in very ultra words
without any latent joke — I don't mean to say at all
that he has unbounded interested reverence for all in
power that his late Suzerain & contemporary before
he long fell.
These are good — particularly, as much severer
satire was well deserved by the little fellow, from the
point from whence these lines came — & was not
omitted from want of ability.
They say "De mortuis nil nisi bonum" therefore I will hold
my tongue.

15. A page from the manuscript of "Salmagundi—aliena, 1834"

16. Anthony Trollope

Claire Clairmont outlived everyone of the Byron-Shelley set. She never softened in her hatred of Byron and continued to regard him as the "murderer" of her child. Soon after the tragedy she travelled to her brother at Vienna and thence to Russia, where she served for some years as a governess. She eventually settled in Florence and in the 1870's converted to Catholicism. For a while she seems to have given some credence to the rumor that her daughter was alive—that Byron had feigned Allegra's death.[5] Claire died in 1879 at the age of eighty. Her epitaph, which she herself wrote, was provocative:

> In misery she spent her life
> expiating not only her faults
> but also her virtues.[6]

Her surviving into old age at Florence provided Henry James with the basis for one of his finest short novels, *The Aspern Papers*: Claire, who lived with a middle-aged spinster niece, was rumored to have valuable Shelley and Byron papers. An American sea captain from Boston named Silsbee, a fanatical collector of Shelley materials, went so far as to arrange lodgings in Claire's house in an effort to obtain the manuscripts. The story went that when Claire died, the niece told Silsbee, "I will give you all the letters if you marry me!" James jotted down the anecdote in his notebook for January 12, 1887, and added: "Certainly there is a little subject there: the picture of the two faded, queer, poor and discredited old English women—living on into a strange generation, in their musty corner of a foreign town—with these illustrious letters their most precious possession."[7] The masterful *Aspern Papers** appeared in the *Atlantic Monthly* for March and May 1888.

Of the leading Harrow principals, Henry Drury died first—in 1841. His nephew, Charles Merivale, said that after Drury's

---

Lion Public House—drink to intoxication—have dice and gambling of various kinds, with other vicious indulgences."[4] Byron would have appreciated the contrasting viewpoints.

* In his fictionalized version, James transferred the scene from Florence to Venice and made his long-dead Romantic poet (Shelley-cum-Byron) an American named Jeffrey Aspern.

bankruptcy in 1827 his health and spirits declined gradually until he "grew prematurely old, dispirited and hopeless, and died of no special ailment at the age of sixty-three."[8] Drury's archrival, J. W. Cunningham, lived on to be Vicar of Harrow through half a century. His influence at Harrow School was somewhat mitigated by the construction—which he vigorously opposed—of a School Chapel in 1839. He became editor of the *Christian Observer* in 1850 and it was this journal which recounted that on Cunningham's death in 1861 "his parishioners followed his body to the grave, like one large family mourning for a father."[9]

Mrs. Trollope prospered. Her literary output was enormous: she worked incessantly from 1832 to 1856, writing 41 books which in their original form ran to some 115 volumes. It is difficult today, when only her first book is widely read, to realize the popularity she once enjoyed and the controversy she provoked. And yet *The New Monthly Magazine* could declare in 1839 that after the publication of *Domestic Manners* "a rapid succession of popular and successful works has confirmed and extended the reputation which her first book achieved; and have won for her an undisputed place amid the principal favourites of the public." The article goes on to say: "Certainly no other author of the present day has been at once so much read, so much admired, and so much abused."[10] After *Domestic Manners* the book which occasioned the most applause and dismay was *The Vicar of Wrexhill* (1837), a heavy-handed attack upon evangelicals. For although Mrs. Trollope did not return to Harrow, she never forgot Cunningham, who was in one way or another the inspiration for the numerous satiric portraits of low church people in her fiction. That Cunningham was the original—however outrageously exaggerated—for the hypocritical and licentious W. Jacob Cartwright of *The Vicar of Wrexhill** cannot be doubted. It was her second most popular book.

* "Wrexhill" was probably derived from Roxeth Hill, an ecclesiastical district of Harrow. Cartwright's initials, W.J.C., vary only slightly from Cunningham's, J.W.C.

After a decade of travelling about Europe and England, Mrs. Trollope in 1844 settled in Florence with her son Thomas Adolphus, the "inseparable companion" of the last thirty years of her life. She died at Florence in 1863 at the age of eighty-three. By that time her other son had eclipsed her.

Anthony Trollope never forgot or forgave the students or masters of Harrow School:

> Something of the disgrace of my school-days has clung to me all through life. Not that I have ever shunned to speak of them as openly as I am writing now, but that when I have been claimed as schoolfellow by some of those many hundreds who were with me either at Harrow or at Winchester, I have felt that I had no right to talk of things from most of which I was kept in estrangement.[11]

The reason old schoolfellows came to "claim" Trollope was of course his fame as a novelist. This great popularity Trollope achieved in the 1860's, when he became, as one contemporary reviewer said, "almost a national institution."[12] But recognition had not come easily or quickly. If we have seen him entertaining literary aspirations and dabbling in poetry at a youthful nineteen, we should recall that only with his fourth novel, *The Warden*, published in 1855 when he was forty, did Trollope find his métier as a writer. Moreover, it was not until five years later with the serialization of *Framley Parsonage* in the first pages of Thackeray's new *Cornhill Magazine* that Trollope attained widespread popularity. These "Barsetshire" novels* have remained Trollope's most well-known. For although many critics today regard the "Palliser" (or "Parliamentary") series as Trollope's supreme achievement, the novel-reading world has always thought the "clerical" stories his best.

It is noteworthy that Trollope, who in his fiction created every variety of cleric, had his first frequent encounters with a

---

* *The Warden* (1855), *Barchester Towers* (1857), *Doctor Thorne* (1858), *Framley Parsonage* (1861), *The Small House at Allington* (1864), and *The Last Chronicle of Barset* (1867).

parish clergyman in the person of J. W. Cunningham. As we have seen, Trollope as a youth talked "a good deal" with Cunningham, and although the Vicar was "always very civil," Trollope considered him "a cringing hypocrite and a most confounded liar," who "would give his eyes to be a bishop." Thus Trollope in 1834. But the mature novelist generally took a broader and more understanding view, even of evangelicals. Not that the low church people of his fiction—Mr. Slope of *Barchester Towers* or the famous Mrs. Proudie of this and other Barsetshire novels—are an attractive lot. But of Mrs. Proudie, for example, Trollope could honestly write: "I shall never be able to make her virtues popular. But she had virtues."[13] And a close reading will prove Trollope correct. He was more tolerant than his mother.

The son also proved more prolific than his remarkable mother. When Anthony died on December 6, 1882 at the age of sixty-seven, he left behind some sixty-six books, including forty-seven novels. Indeed he probably wrote more "good" novels than any other writer in the language.

THE POEMS

LINES WRITTEN
BY A CELEBRATED AUTHORESS
ON THE BURIAL OF THE DAUGHTER
OF A CELEBRATED AUTHOR

1

Twas on the spot, the Muses' favorite haunt,
　　Where gentle Murray,* Phoebus's high priest reigns—
The holy knot whose office 'tis to grant
　　Official answers to his votary's claims,
Assembled sat in divan there to cant,
　　And there to fix the penalties and pains,
Which recreant authors at their hands deserve
　　Who from the laws of Murray's back shop swerve.

2

There full blown loyalty in act to dare
　　Floods like the ladies' fancy in Hyde Park,
And orthodoxy with his virtuous stare
　　Of holy horror at the doctrines dark,
Which with a thunder cloud's portentous glare
　　Threatened a storm to wreck the sacred bark,
That all the tythe laws in its bosom bore,
　　'Twas there he made his stand and prosed for evermore.

---

* John Murray's publishing connection with Byron began with *Childe Harold* in 1812. In that same year Murray moved his firm to 50 Albemarle Street where his "back shop" (as Mrs. Trollope calls it—actually his front drawing room) became a famous literary haunt. At the time of Mrs. Trollope's writing, Murray's literary friends and advisors included Southey, Scott, Gifford, Croker, and various Church of England clergymen. John Murray's descendants still conduct the publishing house at 50 Albemarle Street.

3

In sweet exchange of thoughts legitimate
    The well behaving synod sat most civil:
One praised the bishop's charge, who had of late
    † So clearly proved that knowledge was the evil
Would surest bring destruction to the state,
    And if not checked must lead us to the Devil.
Another made a very neat oration
    To shew that John Bull yet might save the nation.

4

Thus whilst exerting for their country's good,
    The shining talents heaven had lent them all,
A shopman came to Murray as he stood,
    And begged him just to step into the hall,
For that a fellow there was very rude
    Because he had said a package was but small;
For which he charged a most enormous sum,
    'Twas from the Custom house the man had come.

5

Here Murray checked the man in tone severe,
    "Nonsense! the officers of the excise
Are never rude, and never let me hear
    Complaints of men so likely soon to rise:
Let him come in, and it will soon appear
    The value's not proportioned to the size."
Thus Murray spoke in accents douce and loyal,
    For taxes and excise are all but royal.

---

† How some people's politics turn! who would expect that the authoress of _____ _____ that the staunchest of the staunch tories Mrs. _____ [1] would ever have ridiculed such a sentiment as the above. It would now be all that was divine and inspired! Never mind! Southey wrote Wat Tyler.[2]

6

Yet scarce had he these virtuous words spoke,
　Than he repented he had bid them enter,
For on his memory a light there broke,
　Which shewed him, 'twere improvident now to venture,
In presence of so many reverend folk,
　To prosecute the end of the adventure.
So forth he stepped; he should have stepped before,
　The package entered ere he reached the door.

7

Of those who chose bland Murray's skilful hand
　To usher their brains' offspring to the day
Was one, who was not of the canting band,
　One whose wild flights had led him oft astray,
Yet still he was the glory of the land,
　For genius stamped each strange capricious lay,
And kindred genius mourned, when thoughts were found
　That shewed the soaring spirit still earthbound.

8

†But who shall dare that awful mind to scan,
　What earthly censor venture to depart
From the commanded "judge not"? what rash man
　Shall probe the deep wounds of that mighty heart,
Whose secret workings e'en in jesting can
　Make the presumptuous prying gossips start—
The few to whom the light of mind is given
　Feel that that heart can have no judge save heaven.

---

† This is vast nonsense—his Lordship was certainly a clever man—but as selfish a bonvivant as ever lived and no more worthy of the etherial character so often given him than I am. I do not wish to break through that awful "judge not"—but if I were in the habit of doing so—Lord B's case would be no sticking point.

9

This bard was Murray's boast, was Murray's pride,
  Even beyond the riches that he brought,
And lesser names were even set aside,
  Whilst to bring forth his various works he wrought.
Till holy D'Oyly³ clamorously cried
  That all he wrote was greatly worse than naught.
Then sank the spirit of the publisher,
  E'en though the noble author called him dear.

10

Yet not for this did the connexion drop—
  The bard wrote on and Murray published too—
But he grew shier, and was known to stop
  For many minutes thinking what to do,
When came some work, which promised him a crop
  Of reprobation old, and profit new:
For well he knew the public ne'er refused
  To purchase what his pious friends abused.*

11

Shall I amid these stanzas penned in sport,
  In sober sadness, say how fared this bard?
Tell from a source far surer than report
  How deep felt wrongs his better self had marred?

* The casual morality and idiosyncratic liberalism of Byron's poetry had
long disturbed the conservative-thinking Murray. Especially noteworthy
were the first two cantos of *Don Juan*, published in 1819, and *Cain*, in addition to the third, fourth, and fifth cantos of *Don Juan*, published in 1821.
(All five cantos had been issued without the name of either author or
publisher.) Byron's letters to Murray throughout 1822 reflect a growing
impatience with "the most timid of God's booksellers." On June 8, for
example, Byron wrote: "The difference between you and me is, that you
are of *every man's* opinion (especially the last fool's who talks to you), and
I of *no* man's. Both extremes are bad; but we can't establish a medium."
On October 9: "I have no wish to break off our connection, but if you are
to be blown about with every wind, what can I do?" On October 31 he
condemned Murray's "fear of the Parsondom. . . . Admiralty patrons . . .
[and] Quarter*lyers*." By November 18 Byron severed the connection: "I
shall withdraw from you as a publisher, on every account, even on your
own, and I wish you good luck elsewhere."⁴

Till sick of fame where dulness held her court,
  Reckless of hatred, hopeless of regard,
This wayward spirit found a strange delight
  In painting his own portrait black as night.

12

Shame to the Muse that with presumptuous eye
  Should seek in private history to find,
Where only wrinkled beldames ought to pry,
  The secret sorrows of his wondrous mind;
And canting heave the hypocritic sigh
  To all who hate him charitably kind,
Uttering such lays beneath a laurel crown
  As make us wish a butt again might drown.

13

Enough to know he left his native shore
  With no fond consort to beguile the way,
Sought solace in the ocean's sullen roar
  And all unheeded caught its briny spray;
While with eyes backward turned for evermore
  o   o⁵
He gazed towards the land that gave him birth
  And felt himself a wanderer on the earth.

14

Nor can a Muse moral as mine would be
  Recount how he was soothed 'neath other skies.
That man is frail alas we daily see,
  And oft from misery to folly flies.
Nor sinless can he hold himself as free,
  Who at God's altar has formed marriage ties.
—An infant daughter cheered his banished heart,
  Heaven's justice doomed he with this joy should part.

15

Five summers had she clung around his soul,
    And every added year encreased her power,
Each separate grace, the youthful blooming whole
    Crept closer to his heart each passing hour.
And on his mind the clouds that wont to roll
    Were chased as by the sun the passing shower.
This feeling was at least unmixed with sin,
    His Allegra was all his Ada might have been.

16

He saw her sicken and he watched her die,
    The soft small hands' last pressure was his own.
His the last glance of meaning from her eye,
    And his to clasp her when the spark was flown.
Then by her side in anguish down to lie,
    Silent and tearless without sigh or groan.
'Tis not for souls of lesser growth to know
    Of such as his, how deep how strong the woe.

17

Among his early feelings cherished long
    Was one which even malice might have spared;
'Twas the remembrance of affection strong,
    Which in life's joyous morning he had shared
With the blest spirits of the playful throng
    That in thy various frolics with him dared,
Lov'd Harrow—on thy fair and sunny hill,
    Quitted so long, his fancy lingered, still.

18

Now his sick heart found something like relief
    In making there his lost Allegra's grave,
And joyed in cherishing the fond belief,
    That the same spot, his earliest pleasures gave,

Should one day witness his soul's deepest grief,
  He launched the loved remains upon the wave:
As the bark lessened to his aching view,
  The father's spirit seemed departing too—†

19

It was this sad deposit Murray knew
  Was now in act to enter his back shop;
Greatly perplexed he knew not what to do,
  It was too late to tell the man to stop;
And well he guessed how eagerly the crew
  Would catch at every word he might let drop.
He gladly would have formed some specious lie,
  But feared he might offend his friends thereby.

20

A letter too was very plainly seen
  Which in a hurried way he opened straight.
A poet, a smart prebend, and a dean
  Over his shoulder squinted at the date.
Doubtless these gentlemen could never mean
  To read the letter—but 'twas now too late
To lie—So Murray said it was a daughter
  Lord B had sent to him across the water.

21

Send you a daughter Murray in a cask?
  What daughter? Is't a daughter of his brain?
Poor Murray! truly 'twas no easy task,
  The strange mysterious business to explain.
But to reply to all that they should ask
  Were, he soon found, an undertaking pain.
So shortly as he could he told the tale
  Which had been sent him by the last week's mail.

---

† Query: was the father a brandy merchant?

22

The tale was doubtless strange, but it was true,
  Yet not for that was it the more believed—
"A likely story to make such ado,
  And does he think the world will be deceived?
I rather guess that he will find but few
  By whom this wild romance will be received.
No no—we know my Lord a little better,—
  But Murray prithee let us see the letter."

23

This Murray said he could not shew to any,
  But Doctor someone proved that he was wrong;
"For though," said he, "I would not give a penny
  For all that he could write in prose or song,
Yet still I think it may do good to many
  To expose the man they have admired so long."
Then Murray shewed the letter to a few:
  Alas! poor Murray! what else could he do.

24

Then in full chorus from all voices burst
  One horror toned prodigious virtuous cry:
"Depraved" "profane" "adulterous" "vile" "accursed"
  In various notes of canting reached the sky.
And each among them tried to be the first
  Some dreadful hidden motive to descry.
Not one among them felt the slightest doubt
  That some there were, could they but find it out.

25

So forth they passed—each eager to reveal
  To his own chosen circle of dear friends,
All they had promised Murray to conceal,
  And not a few that evening were the pens

That hastily dispatched a glorious meal
 Of what the city to the country lends—
New spite—new gossip—and a few new lies
 To cheer their country neighbors' hearts and eyes.

26

Thus having bowed them off Murray remained
 Alone, with the strange package at his feet.
Now to speak truth he had felt somewhat pained
 By all the yelling he had heard, replete
As 'twas with malice—but he had gained
 Their thanks for what he'd given them to repeat.
For a bel-esprit can have no possession†
 Which helps him on so much in his profession.

27

Now his next care was with despatch to send,
 As his instructions specially directed,
Notice of this arrival to a friend,[6]
 Who for this mournful task had been selected,
Begging his prompt assistance he would lend
 To have the bones by holy earth protected.
'Twas with no pomp of funeral array
 That the fair infant joined her kindred clay.

28

A simple shrine memorial of her name
 The mourning father wished erected near.
No line of his from whom a word is fame
 Was on the humble tablet to appear.
'Twas but to mark, when near the spot he came
 To dew her grave with a paternal tear,
That there his lovely Allegra was laid,
 That there his heart's fond tribute must be paid.

---

† What possession this means is not evident. I suppose
malice—but it is only a guess—perspicuity of style is by
no means one of the merits of this poem.

29

Ascend my Muse upon a bolder wing,
  'Tis no mere earthly tale I would unfold:
Bear me aloft, that I may fitly sing
  Not of the worn out Goddesses of old,
Who to my verse could no attention bring—
  I sing a new one, but of late enrolled
Beneath the wide Pantheon of the sky,
  Thence let her now descend to meet a mortal's eye.

30

Almighty Cant—let my song reach to thee,
  'Tis thy omniscience I would gladly shew,
Thou, who if rightly worshipped can set free
  From every   o⁷ else thy slaves below.
Fain for thy glory would I let men see
  How much to thee thy fervent votaries owe.
And also awful Goddess I would say
  What the mild duty is that they must pay.

31

'Tis thine to fill the empty heart with zeal,
  The zeal of seeming just what it is not.
How many at thy bidding lowly kneel,
  When thou dost shew them, something's to be got.
What pious ardour do thy votaries feel
  For this or that creed—'tis no matter what.
Thou givest the key—thy children's mouths all ope
  In praise of Calvin, Luther or the Pope.

32

Turn thy inspiring visage to the South,
  It teems with pardons, penances and masses.
Let the North feel a zephyr from thy mouth,
  "The church's in danger" bray the docile asses.

Then smile aside and lo! behold a growth
    Of slaves whose ardour all the rest surpasses.
To please thee, they will rant and roar and rave,
    And swear to all that thou alone canst save.

33

And thou art not ungrateful, thou dost bring
    Assured success to all that worship thee.
To one thou dost a golden mitre fling,
    Another gets a borough as his fee.
Whilst those the loudest in thy chorus sing,†
    We highest on promotion's ladder see.
Nor Justice 'self with nicer hand can weigh
    Degrees of merit, or more fairly pay.

34

Such Goddess is thy universal power!
    Fain would I now in humble accents say,
How lately in thy most auspicious hour,
    Towards Harrow hill thou late didst take the way,
And choosing from among her sons the flower,
    Thou marshallest them around in fair array.
Within their vestry where most folks agree
    They not infrequently are met by thee.

35

It was thy special care that brought them there
    Upon a business that was quite thine own:
And as they entered with parental care
    In which thy earnest zeal for it was shewn,

---

† These two lines are unintelligible at present—the
meaning is—Whilst those, the loudest in the choirs [sic]
who sing &c. It must have the relative.[8]

Thou placed thyself, where best thou couldst prepare
    (†To) Each favorite son to make thy power known.
And breathed such shining influence around,
    That all who entered felt 'twas holy ground.

36

Thy mantling veil about thee widely thrown
    What was unseemly did conceal from sight,
But thy raised eye, and drawn down mouth were shewn,
    Those eyes that seemed like innocence—all white.
That mouth which looked, as (if‡) it had never known
    To smile or utter any feeling light.
Grave was thy bearing, solemn was thy face,
    Whilst every movement shewed some holy grace.

37

And like a vision round thee floated still
    Shadows of loaves and fishes wondrous fair,
Which thou didst render mobile at thy will,
    Making them move around thee here and there,
To meet each comer as in act to fill
    His gaping mouth with something rich and rare.
No sprite of upper air greets men below
    Who has so many promised joys to shew.

38

Thy voice had summoned and thy votaries came,
    The order of their march I cannot say,
But I would fain tho' without order name
    Those that did then and there their homage pay.

---

† There is no "*to*" in the copy from which I took this
—it is my own putting in—it is nonsense without—and
very bad with it.

‡ "*if*" is absolutely necessary here—it is neither sense
or grammar without it.

And if I could, would consecrate to fame
    Each pious word that uttered was that day.
But to do this would too much swell my tale,
    Their eloquence I therefore must curtail.

39

†Black letter Harry, deep in classic lore,
    Whose ample front speaks frankness and good sense,
He who in strange variety can pore
    With drudging patience over mood and tense,
And join anon the table's social roar,
    The wittiest of the set with least pretence,
The Roxburgher⁹ of all the crew was he,
    Who joins most learning with the frankest glee.

40

‡He stood apart nor owned the Goddess' power
    Yet sometimes he would listen to her too.
And I have heard that in an evil hour
    He has been known to laud the pensioned crew.

---

† These lines on old Harry are not bad. I don't know that his ample front speaks frankness and good sense—his frankness is bearishness—but he is a good natured fellow—though he has often nearly plagued my life out. He is truly "a black letter toper of port," as a certain poet whose name we won't mention says of him.¹⁰

‡ The fair authoress mixes up Toryism and Cant in rather a singular and unjust manner—but she has learnt her errors by this time. Old Harry has as little cant as any man I know—but he is apt to praise the pensioned crew in very ultra words without any latent joke—I don't mean to say at all that he has unbounded, interested reverence for all in power that his late Suzerain and contemporary, Doctor Butler, felt.

And speak with great respect of all in power,
   And say that mischief lurked in what was new.
But yet I much believe some latent joke
   Lay shrouded in the ultra words he spoke.

41

Before him stood looking most wondrous wise
   The worthy little Evans[11] of the vale.
His was no start of makebelieve surprise,
   When as he listened to the wondrous tale,
He opened wide his horror stricken eyes,
   And blessed his stars that he was not so frail.
For he was sure not all the world could say
   He'd quitted Mrs Evans night or day.†

42

Next ‡Mills[12] with great propriety of face,
   And really meaning to be very right,
Entered the vestry, with no more grimace
   Than those must use who mean for Cant to fight,

---

† These are good—particularly as much severer satire was well deserved by this little fellow, from the point from whence these lines came—and was not omitted from want of ability.
They say "De mortuis nil nisi bonum." Therefore I will hold my tongue.

‡ This is a capital picture of Mills. I used always to stick up for Mills—I don't know why—for he is a weak, quarrelsome, conceited ass—not to speak of his absolute vulgarity and ignorance. He has always a most laughable mode of keeping up his dignity, and walks with his nose ludicrously in the air. He had the upper shell[13] when I was in that part—he used constantly to make bad puns on the boys' names. When Evans died old Harry was made under master but still kept the 5th form instead of taking the third as usual, as Mills was too much of an ass. He—Mills—has now I believe left Harrow, and got a school in Exeter.

And with discretion took a forward place
  Where all that passed would be within his sight.
He looked around with an important air
  And seemed well pleased he had been summoned there.

43

And Batten†¹⁴ too arrived who had he not
  Been cloud wrapt in the Goddess' murky arm
And underneath her banners always fought,
  When she was near enough to shew her charm,
Had worthy been of much higher lot
  Than quietly to echo these alarms.
Sincere are many who to cant begin,
  Wishing to be too good was Batten's greatest sin.

44

With careless smile, loud jocund William‡¹⁶ near,
  He recked but little what they were about,
Till hints he heard, which roused a sudden fear,
  That the affair might make a serious rout

---

† Poor Batten was dead before I went to Harrow the second time, but I recollect him as the most good natured fellow I ever knew—he certainly had no Cant about his manner; excepting Kennedy¹⁵—the man who now occupies the house which Batten had—Batten I suppose was the cleverest master Harrow ever had, and the most learned—although he had not perhaps so much classic lore about him as Harry Drury.

‡ Jocund William and his father Mark Drury¹⁷ were obliged to run away from their creditors at Harrow a short time after this was written. They now live at Brussels where William has a church and a school. Speaking of these two prize clergymen, and Mark's nephew—Harry—whom we spoke of before—the same poet says in allusion to their size
  "If he and his uncle and cousin
    Who payed but two pence in the pound

Among the school boys' parents far and near,
On which his virtue too began to sprout,
And in his turn he made a short oration
On laws, religion and our prosperous nation.

45

And now among them entered with an air
Of dignity and hurry strangely blended,
One who 'twas plain thought himself master there,
Though to be condescending he intended,
And in their business piously to share,
For no one than himself was more offended
At this most dreadful threatened profanation,
Which of the church was open violation.

46

Alas! tis pity, Butler,[18] sooth to speak,
Thine eye that might have power to dare the day,
Should favour, patronage, protection seek,
And counterfeit respect and homage pay,
With an anxiety that pales thy cheek
And early turns thy raven locks to gray.
Nature intended thee for something better,
Than for a Lordling's smile to live a debtor.

47

Why dost thou bend so low when rank is near?
Why are thy better feelings set to sleep?
Should Lord or Bishop frown,—what dost thou fear?
Thy mind can soar, then let not thine heart creep,

Were weighed against any two dozen
They'd soon find their way to the ground."
Arthur Drury, William's brother, my old master at Sunbury is larger than either—well may it be said that he
made a short oration, for at that time he stuttered so
much, that he could not have made a long one, altho he
sometimes preached.

†Seek not to all in power to appear
  Bound to their cause with such devotion deep,
Abandon once for all the canting plan,
  Value thy self and dare to be a man.‡

48

Next entering from the church, where as 'twas thought,
  He had in private prayed a little prayer,
The mild eyed vicar§ to the vestry brought
  The graces of the Goddess who reigned there;
And with her own soft tone and action sought
  To shew of all their souls his pious care.
In truth he was the Goddess' darling son,
  And as she gave him utterance, he begun.

---

† These lines are bad, 1st—because power is properly only one syllable. 2nd because—the words are twisted about so much, and as their refers to power, it should be in a separate division of the sentence—at least, wherever the fault lies—there is one somewhere, as it is very obscure.

‡ As to Butler—I recollect very little of him except that tho' he was very severe to little boys, he was a very inefficient master—and the school went on declining till he resigned[19]—he was altogether unable to keep the head boys in order, and rather feared them, than was feared by them.

§ Cunningham the vicar—he may well be called "mild eyed"—a man almost worshipped by the low church at Harrow, very unpopular with the gentry, and much feared by the poor—a most despicable hypocrite— a gentleman like man with very pleasing manners and a sweet voice. I used to talk to Cunningham a good deal at one time, and recall he always used to be very civil to me, but he is a cringing hypocrite and a most confounded liar, and would give his eyes to be a bishop, which he was nearly being [sic] at one time, I believe, but it was only of one of the colonies.

49

"Dear friends, dear fellow sinners, we are here
   I hope in very friendly council met
To speak upon a point to all most dear,
   And God forbid that any one should let
In this cause any difference appear.
   It would be lasting subject of regret,
Should we give room to anyone to say
   We were not all of one accord today.

50

"It is indeed a very shocking thing,
   That one who is so very great a man
Should such disgrace upon our parish fling:
   To send the infant hither was a plan
Which could not fail much injury to bring,
   But by my preaching I'll do all I can
To counteract the influence of the bones
   Unhappily now laid beneath our stones.

51

"But this is done so no more can be said.
   What now demands your most mature advice
Is, whether o'er the ashes of the dead
   I should consent to place at any price
A stone on which the child's name may be read.
   †*May it not lead the school boys into vice?*
This is a question that concerns us all,
   And the importance of it is not small.

---

† This question was actually asked—and the reason given for not putting up a tablet to the memory of Allegra, Lord Byron's natural daughter, in Harrow Church, was for fear it should teach the boys to get bastards.

52

"I own I think there is great likelihood,
　That such may be the lamentable case.
And much I fear, if rightly understood,
　This was the reason why he chose this place,
Or else it was, because in pious mood
　His lady[20] hither sometimes turns for grace,
Or he might mean chiefly to vex me
　Because he knows my spotless purity.

53

"But yet I should by no means think it right
　This great man's noble talents to deny,
Indeed I own I was delighted quite,
　When Cain* that great performance met my eye:
And should you, Mr Drury, chance to write
　To your accomplished friend, I wish that my
Great admiration of the genius shewn
　In that performance should to him be known."†

---

† Mr C. actually said this to Harry Drury. Harry's answer was "Do you indeed—I think it the most blasphemous production that ever came from the press."

* *Cain*, in which the reader could not help but see Byron's sympathy for Lucifer (a soul who could "look the Omnipotent tyrant in/ His everlasting face, and tell him that/ His evil is not good" I, i, 137-40), caused great critical outcry: J. G. Lockhart in *Blackwoods* wrote that "taken altogether, [Cain] is a wicked and blasphemous performance, destitute of any merit sufficient to overshadow essential defects of the most abominable nature." An anonymous reviewer for the *Gentleman's Magazine* called the work "unquestionably one of the most pernicious productions that ever proceeded from the pen of a man of genius. It is in fact neither more nor less than a series of wanton libels upon the Supreme Being and His attributes." Jeffrey in the *Edinburgh Review* said that in spite of some beautiful and powerful passages he had to "regret very much that [Cain] should ever have been published. It will give great scandal and offence to pious persons in general—and be the means of suggesting painful doubts and distressing perplexities, to hundreds of minds that might never otherwise have been exposed to such dangerous disturbance." Shelley, on the other hand, wrote: "*Cain* is apocalyptic—it is a revelation not before communicated to man."[21]

54

Then the rich army agent,† Campbell, rose,
  With vehemence of virtuous feeling warm;
Hurling his Scotch thunder upon those,
  Who dared to doubt the threatened stone could harm.
Furious with chastity, prepared for blows,
  He challenged all the vestry round to arm,
If any 'mongst them could so vile be found
  To mark a bastard's grave on Christian ground.

55

"I cannot, gentlemen, indeed believe,
  Though I confess I'm vera much surprised,
That you the bastard's body should receive,
  I cannot think ye'll be sa ill advised
As such a horrid project to conceive,
  As never yet by Christian was devised,
Ye will not, will ye, set a mickle stane
  To mark the spot that does her dust contain.

56

"By heaven, gentlemen, an if ye do,
  I'll shew the world how I despise ye all—
I ne'er again will enter my own pew,
  Or bring my virtuous daughters great and small,
Lest their pure eyes the horrid sight should view,
  Of this cursed tablet placed against the wall.
For (‡now) what else can ye expect I pray,
  But that the school will do the same next day."

---

† Campbell, in the year 30, went smash—both in his face and fortune—how many smashes we have had in Harrow. Campbell proved himself a blackguard.[22]

‡ now is an interpolation of my own—a mere expletive to give metre, and often used in that way by Scotch and Irish orators.

57

"Indeed Sir you have harped my fears aright,"
　　Observed the Doctor with a flattering bow,
"I see the thing exactly in this light,
　　That I must feel most anxious, you'll allow
The eternal interests of my pupils might
　　Be hazarded—were we not steady now.
I must in short insist on it that here
　　No tablet so disgraceful should appear."†

58

Oh it is nauseous—I can‡ write no more—
　　These are the orgies, Cant, that thou dost claim,
Such the libations that thy votaries pour
　　Upon thy altar—while no touch of shame
Has pained e'en those who when they passed the door,
　　Would all commerce in such stuff disdain.
Does one among them think the joys of heaven
　　Will be as meed of utter fooling given?

59

So much for Cant—and now one word for thee,
　　Thou half oppressed and well nigh stifled power,
In thy adversity more dear to me
　　Than if no cloud did o'er thy beauty lower.

---

† All this is really true—and an assembly of learned men at Harrow agreed that a tablet should not be placed to the memory of Allegra Byron—for fear of injuring the boys' chastity—of course the Drurys had nothing to do with it.

‡ There is quite enough already and to spare—had it been condensed it would have been better—the latter part about the masters is very clever, true, and well put. I shewed these lines to W Drury, one of the party at Brussels.

Ill treated virtue—'tis a grief to see
   The light thou givest us weakning every hour,
Because a base usurper takes thy place,
   And for thy glorious truth gives us her foul grimace.

60

But is it just, thou banished poet, say,
   Because this base usurper takes her name,
That virtue's self should suffer in thy lay?
   'Tis such as thou shouldst vindicate her fame,
And drag the whining hypocrites to day
   Who under colours false her honors claim.
When maudlin moralists begin to teach,
   How many doze rather than hear them preach.†

61

But mighty bard turn *but* thy powers aright,
   And who shall match thee in thine high career,
Sublime, pathetic, sportive in thy might,
   How glorious couldst thou make the right appear.
Dart through thy verse a ray of holy light,
   And make the coward Tartuffes quake with fear.
'Tis such as thou that to savage vice may dare,
   Nor fear that Cant shall catch thee in her snare.‡

---

† Twaddle all this—the last line very absurd.

‡ Finis—this is an eccentric idea—this of setting up Byron as the champion of virtue—but admiration does wonders. There is much wit in the lampoon, and it is interesting to me from a variety of causes.

F I N I S

OTHER POEMS IN ANTHONY TROLLOPE'S
"SALMAGUNDI"

RS. Trollope's satire is the third of four poems written out in Anthony's "Salmagundi." The other poems, reproduced below, are considerably shorter than his mother's. The first, "The Two Veterans," satirizes the Prince Regent on the occasion of the festivities which celebrated the "definitive" defeat of Napoleon in 1814. For two weeks in mid-June London wildly cheered the victors and entertained potentates from all Europe. Alexander I of Russia and Frederick William II of Prussia headed the list of distinguished visitors, but it was the Prussian military hero, old Marshal Blücher, who most captured the public's fancy. The official host, the Prince Regent, was constantly embarrassed by the untimely appearances of his estranged wife, Princess Caroline. The populace generally favored Caroline, and the Regent was hissed in public.

"The Two Veterans" appeared anonymously in the *Morning Chronicle* of June 29, 1814. Trollope wrote, "I think it is by Moore. It is his stile." Thomas Moore did indeed write lampoons of this kind for the *Morning Chronicle*, but he was not the only one to do so, and there is not sufficient evidence to declare the poem his work. Moore was not in London for the festivities, although he did ask Samuel Rogers for details "of all that has been *ridiculous* (for *that* is the best part, after all) in these shows and ceremonies. How does 'our fat friend' [Beau Brummell's words for the Prince Regent] go on? among all these fighting chieftains, he seems particularly to distinguish himself in what is called *fighting shy. Is* he or is he *not* hissed wherever he goes?"[1]

The second poem in Trollope's collection, "Lines by Lady Caroline Lamb," recalls the most famous of Byron's many liaisons. Caroline, who married William Lamb in 1805, had long been wild and capricious but this eccentricity was greatly aggravated by contact with Byron. Upon first meeting him in March, 1812, she wrote in her diary, "mad—bad—and dangerous to know."[2] Their affair lasted only a few months. Her indiscretions displeased both society and Byron: she presented herself, often disguised as a page, in his rooms at all hours; she waited outside in the street for him; she suffered hysterically over him. Meanwhile, Byron's attentions wandered: he proposed to and was refused by Caroline's husband's cousin, Anne Isabella Milbanke; he became fascinated by Caroline's mother-in-law, Lady Melbourne; and he took up with Lady Oxford. By November Byron formally dismissed Caroline: "our affections are not in our own power—mine are engaged. I love another."[3] At her country home at Brocket Caroline had a group of young girls dance around a fire as she burned Byron's effigy and copies—not the originals—of his letters to her. In July of 1813 she met Byron at a party and caused great commotion by attempting to use a knife on herself. In 1816, at the time of Byron's separation from his wife, Caroline was probably the one who spread the rumors of the poet's incest with his half-sister Augusta. Shortly thereafter Caroline published a novel, *Glenarvon*, an undisguised account of her affair with Byron. The book was a three-week's wonder in London. Byron's comment was: "As for the likeness, the picture can't be good—I did not sit long enough."[4] Lady Caroline, outcast from society, wrote more novels, published some poetry, had a number of desperate and pathetic love affairs, and suffered various mental and physical breakdowns (one occasioned by an accidental meeting with the funeral procession of Byron in July, 1824). As death from illness neared, Caroline apparently became repentant and embraced religious sentiments. She died in January, 1828.

The authorship of "Lines by Lady Caroline Lamb" is unknown. The reference at the end, "In Journal Vol IV p 42" is to Trollope's own destroyed journal of the 1830's, and it is possible that he himself composed this poem, although the *aliena* of his title suggests "[poems or works] belonging to others." (On the other hand, *aliena* can also mean "hostile, unfriendly, unfavorable.") The final item in the "Salmagundi," an untitled, cynical, seize-the-day poem on love, is also of unknown authorship.

THE TWO VETERANS†

Hectora quem laudas pro te pugnare jubeto,
Militia est operis altera digna tuis.—Ovid*

Oh! Wine is the thing to make Veterans tell
Of their deeds and their triumphs—and punch does as well.
As the R–g—t and Blucher, that sober old pair,
Fully proved t'other night, when they supped, you know where,
And good humouredly bragged of the feats they'd been doing,
O'er exquisite punch of Y-arm—th's** own brewing.
This difference there was in the modes of their strife,
One had fought with the *French—t'other* fought with his *wife!*
"How I dressed them" says Blucher, and filled up sublime,
"I too" says the Prince, "have dressed men in my time."
Bl. "One morning at dawn—"
Reg. "Zounds how early you fight!
I could never be ready— (*hiccups*) my things are so tight!"
Bl. "I sent forward a few pioneers over night—"
Reg. "Ugly animals these are, in general I hear— (*hiccups*)
The Q————n⁶ you must know is my chief pioneer."
Bl. "The foe came to meet us—"
Reg.   "There I manage better,
    The foe would meet me, but I'm d————d if I'll let her."
Bl. "Pell Mell was the word—dash thro' thick and thro' thin—"
Reg. "C-rlt-n House⁷ to a tittle! how well we chime in!"
Bl. "For the fate of all Europe, the fate of men's rights
    We battled—"

---

† The Two Veterans—from the Morning Chronicle. Written at the time, when the great fête was given at Whites⁵ to all the potentates then in England. I think it is by Moore. It is his stile.

* "Bid Hector, whom you praise, go warring in your stead; 'tis the other campaigning befits your prowess" *Heroides* XVII, 255-56 (Grant Showerman translation).
** Lord Yarmouth, later Third Marquis of Hertford (1777-1842), influential associate of and vice chamberlain to the Regent; known for his corrupt and luxurious life style, Hertford was the original for Lord Steyne in Thackeray's *Vanity Fair* and for Lord Monmouth in Disraeli's *Coningsby*.

Reg. "And I for the grand fête at White's!"
Bl. "Though ways deep and dirty delayed our design—"
Reg. "Never talk of the dirt of *your* ways—think of *mine*!"
Bl. "And the balls hissing round—"
Reg. "Oh! those balls be my lot,
Where a good supper is, and the Pr-nc-ss is not.
And for hissing—why, faith, I've so much every day,
That my name, I expect, in the true royal way,
Will descend to Posterity, 'George le Sifflé.' "[8]
Bl. "But we conquered, we conquered—blest hour of my life!"
Reg. "And blest moment of mine, when I conquered my wife!"
Here the dialogue faltered—he still strove to speak—
But strong was the Punch, and the R———t's head weak;
And the Marshal cried "Charge!" and the bumpers went
    round—
Till the fat toilet-veteran sunk on the ground.
And old Blucher triumphantly crowed from his seat,
To see one worthy Potentate more at his feet!

LINES BY LADY CAROLINE LAMB

If thou couldst know what 'tis to weep,
   To weep unpitied and alone,
The live long night, whilst others sleep,
Silent and mournful watch to keep,
   Thou wouldst not do, what I have done.

If thou couldst know what 'tis to smile,
   To smile whilst scorned by every one,
To hide by many an artful wile,
A heart that knows more grief than guile,
   Thou wouldst not do, what I have done.

And oh! if thou couldst think how drear,
   When friends are changed, and health is gone,
The world would to thine eyes appear,
If thou like me to none wert dear,
   Thou wouldst not do what I have done.

In Journal Vol IV p 42.
Her husband—Lord Melbourne—is at present premier.
August 1834.

[WHY ART THOU SO MELANCHOLY?]

Why art thou so melancholy?
Dost thou love? 'tis idle folly!
Woulds't thou have thy Sacharissa?
         Kiss her.

If with proud repulsive glances,
She does meet thy warm advances,
When thou dost again caress her,
         Press her!

Should her scornful frown grow blacker,
While thou fondly dost attack her,
Nothing will the girl enamour,
         Damn her.

APPENDIX

MRS. TROLLOPE'S ANTI-EVANGELICAL
VERSE DRAMA

AMONG the Trollope family papers in the University of Illinois Library is a manuscript in an unidentified hand which preserves three one-act verse dramas by Mrs. Trollope. These satiric plays, written in couplets of iambic pentameter, were obviously intended for home entertainment. Reproduced below is the one most germane to this study, "Signs of the Times, or, The Righteous Rout," yet another attack upon evangelicals. (The others, "Almacks, or, The Alarm" and "Meeting of the Friends of Mutation," satirize the grand entertainments given by ladies of rank and the would-be conspiracies of political revolutionaries.)

"The Signs of the Times" was probably written in the early or mid 1830's. The remark of one of the evangelical characters, "If, as you hope, we have secured the throne," suggests a reference to William IV, who had to make accommodations to the Whigs.

The play has marked similarities to Mrs. Trollope's widely-read and controversial novel of 1837, *The Vicar of Wrexhill*. Indeed, as is indicated in the notes below, two "poems" from "The Signs of the Times" were inserted into the novel. But more importantly, in both the light-hearted play and the all-too-serious novel, Mrs. Trollope underscored what she despised in evangelicalism: hypocritical disdain for pleasure, anti-intellectualism, toadying to rich benefactors, unscrupulous ecclesiastical ambition. In addition, and quite predictably, the play's Reverend Mr. Fripp, with his unctuous talk, devoted female disciples, adoring daughters, interest in missionary societies, and fawning attitude towards the bishop, unmistakably calls to mind Mrs. Trollope's old obsession, J. W. Cunningham.

SIGNS OF THE TIMES,

OR,

THE RIGHTEOUS ROUT

Scene: the Reverend Mr Fripp's drawing room. The Rev^d Mr Fripp, The Revd Mrs Fripp and the Revd Miss Fripps

Mr Fripp *(looking at his watch)*

'Tis nearly eight—our friends tonight are late,
I hope, my dear, they will not make us wait
For that pure source of social christian's glee,
The not inebriating, but cheering tea.

Mrs Fripp

I look for none but servants of the Lord,
No danger such should ever break their word.
Eight was the hour all promised to be here,
And ere St. George's strikes they will appear.

(Enter footman with a note, which he delivers to Mr Fripp. The ladies approach very closely to him.)

Miss M Fripp

The Lord I trust will guard his own from ill,
But we submit in all things to his will!
Say, dear Papa!—can't Mr Busby come?

Miss P Fripp

More likely, Mary, 'tis from Mr Shumm,
Thrice on last Sunday did he preach the word,
Last night I know he wrestled with the Lord.
He told me that he felt the flesh was frail,
And as he spoke he turned from red to pale;
For his great soul, his body was too weak!
'Tis he that cannot come—Papa, pray speak.

Mr. Fripp *(gently pushing them back with one hand, and holding the note out of their reach with the other.)*

My blessed lambs I read the note aloud. *(Reads)*
"May I, dear sir, this evening be allowed
"To bring my pupil, Mr Edward Combe,
"To join the circle in your drawing room?
"His wealthy pious father has consigned

"His son to me that I may lead his mind,
"From human learning unto heavenly grace,
"I trust it will not prove a desperate case,
"Though I confess there's something in the lad,
"That shews him either reprobate, or mad.
"But for his soul there's nothing I can do
"So good as letting him drink tea with you."

Mrs Fripp

Oh! that must be from blessed Mr Jay,
You need not write, me dear ————

Mr Fripp

No (*to the footman*) only say
We shall be glad to see the young man here.
                    (*Knocking*)
Go to the door, John—you were right my dear,
'Tis not quite eight, but those who serve the Lord,
As you so well remark, ne'er break their word.

(*Enter Lady Diana Finch and the Rev*ᵈ *Mr Aimwell. They all
press on another's hands and smile very sweetly, while Lady
Diana begins these words.*)

Lady Diana

My dear good friends! Oh! it is joy of heart
In such society to bear a part.
I know my sins were grievous to the Lord,
But that he'll wash his own, we have his word.
Oh! blessed be the providential care,
That made me seek for joy where good men are.
How nearly had my sinful soul been wrecked.
Dear blessed friends!—Whom else do you expect?

Mr Fripp

Some most distinguished of the chosen few
Who have exchanged the old man for the new;
Midst these your Ladyship need not be told,
Mr Achmuty the chief place must hold.

Lady Di

Mr Achmuty, blessed pious man!

Mrs Fripp

Good Mr Aimwell, have you seen our plan
For a branch missionary child's committee?

Miss Phoebe

Oh Mr Aimwell! 'tis so sweetly pretty,
To see each saintly little angel come,
Holding between its finger and its thumb
The halfpenny that once was spent in sin.
(Knocking)

Mr Fripp

When these friends enter we'll our tea begin:
Expounding to the school has made me dry.

Miss Mary

Yes, dear Papa—and dining on goose-pie!

(Enter Mr Achmuty, Miss Rose Achmuty, and the hon^{ble} Mr Wilson. After them, Mr Jay, Mr E Combe, Mr Busby, and Mr Shumm.)

Mr Achmuty

My excellent good friends—come we too late?
I've been considering last night's debate.
And sat so long with my friend Wilson here,
That we have pass'd the promis'd hour, I fear.

(All crowd round him with marks of devotionate admiration.)

Mr Fripp

Your time, dear sir, belongeth to the Lord,
And he will give your labours their reward.
For me, I hold myself among the blest,
When providence vouchsafes me such a guest.
Good Mr Wilson! worthy Mr Jay!
My dear, Miss Rose, I hope you're well to-day.
My much esteem'd good friend, is this the youth,
Whom you would lead into the path of truth?
Young man! may you henceforward grow in grace,
And win in time the godly christian race.

(They all sit down. Tea is handed round, of which they all partake largely, excepting Mr E Combe who makes wry faces at it, upon which John sighs deeply.)

Lady Di

How far unlike is this dear blessed tea,
To the gay fêtes which once delighted me!
I shared no converse then devout and holy;
Ah!—all was wit and sin and taste of folly.

Mr Jay

    Alas! my Lady, poetry and song
    Were what the tempter used to lead you wrong,
    But you have proved that it was useless all.

Mr Achmuty

    Yours my dear Lady was a splendid call.
    Nor can we doubt that all the host of heaven
    Thanks to the saints on earth for you have given,
    Desperate indeed I once believ'd your case,
    Nothing had saved your soul but God's especial grace.

Mr Aimwell

    His name be praised therefore!

All

    Amen! Amen!

Mr E Combe

    Was Lady Di so sad a sinner then,
    When first from her while yet an Eton boy,
    I learnt to taste of intellectual joy?
    Left fives and cricket for the Tuscan bard,
    Out-watched the moon to merit her regard!
    Nor through the lustre that has since pass'd by
    Have I forgot her cheering prophecy
    Of what I might be—Such perhaps I am,
    Yet dare not conjugate the verb to DAMN.
    Till I do that through every mood and tense,
    To her approval now I've no pretense.

Mrs Fripp

            Horrible!

Mr Busby

            Tremendous!

John

                  Oh!

Mr Jay

    'Tis sad to hear a christian youth speak so.

Mr Achmuty

    At least young man you cannot but confess,
    We teach to conjugate the verb to bless.

Mr E Combe (*laughing*)

    Yes—the first persons, and the passive voice.

Mr Achmuty

    Oh! Mr Jay, how would my heart rejoice,

    Could the keen wit of this poor sinful youth

    Be won to aid the cause of grace and truth.

                (whispers to Mr Jay)

    His father is—pious—and rich you say

              (aloud—pointing to Miss Rose)

    Present us to your pupil, Mr Jay.

Mr Jay

    Miss Rose Achmuty—Mr Edward Combe.

Miss Rose

    Will you sit here, Sir? Phoebe will make room.

    Perhaps her album you would like to see,

    Which she was showing Mr Shumm, and me.

(Mr Combe sits down between the young ladies, who offer to his notice the choicest treasure of the album. He takes the volume, and reads in a low voice the table of contents.)

    Saint Paul's head, sketched in pen and ink;[1]

    "Fly not yet" to words of grace;

    The death bed talk of Master Blink;

    Lines on a fallen virgin's case;

    Sonnet upon heavenly love;

    A pencil drawing of Saint Peter;

    Emblems—The pigeon and the dove;

    Gray's ode turned to psalm-tune metre;

    A christian ode in praise of tea,

    Freely translated from Redi.[2]

(Whilst he reads, enter the Bishop of Allfaith.)

Mr Fripp *(stepping eagerly forward, and seizing his hands)*

    My Lord! my dearest Lord! Thanks be to heaven

    That to our heavenly prayers this grace hath given.

(To John, who stands gazing at the Bishop with the door in his hand)

    Bring fresh hot tea, and muffins also hot.

(Presenting the Bishop to the company)

    Oh! my dear friends, how blessed is that man's lot,

    Who can a real Christian Bishop see!

    You all will join to praise the Lord with me.

Mr Combe (*aside to Miss Phoebe*)
　　What Lord is that your father's praising now?
Miss Phoebe (*aside to Mr Combe*)
　　Dear Mr Combe!—you're very odd, I trow.
The Bishop (*smiling all around and squeezing the hand of Lady
Diana, the humble Mr Wilson, and Mr Achmuty*)
　　The peace and grace of God be with you all!
(*looking earnestly at Mr Combe*)
　　Who's that young man? Has he yet had a call?
　　Me thinks this world is written on his face.
Mr Jay (*looking alarmed*)
　　My Lord he comes to me to look for grace.
Bishop
　　I trust he'll find it, Sir——
　　　　　　　　　　　　(*to Mr Achmuty*)
　　　　　　　　　　My valuable friend,
　　How did last night's debate in your house end?
Mr Achmuty
　　We'd no division, my beloved Lord,
　　But many spoke with fervour for the word.
　　Daily I think our house improves in grace,
　　Though still vile ribaldry pollutes the place.
Mr Aimwell (*smiling*)
　　Why yes in truth there's many a "parlous knave"
　　Who aims more to be witty than to save.
Bishop (*gravely to Mr Aimwell*)
　　Beware young man of loose citations—ne'r
　　Pollute discourse with such—they are a snare,
　　Spread by the foul one.
Mr Aimwell
　　Sir—I stand reproved.
The Bishop (*smiling again very graciously*)
　　You take reproof, Sir, as a young man should,
　　(*to Mr Achmuty*)
　　Yes my good friend, I think it doth appear,
　　That Providence begins to interfere.
　　The Lord perceives there are some Saints on earth,
　　Who merit he should put his power forth.

Behold the effect of preaching—near thee,
Some names must not be named, but all agree
A call or something very like a call,
              (whispers to Mr Achmuty)

Mr Achmuty *(solemnly)*
      Therein the Lord at once rewards us all.

Bishop
      Yes, Sir, the Lord is active—but beware
      That we for this do not our labour spare,
      The more the vineyard is seen to thrive,
      The more th'encouraged husbandman should strive.
      Satan is active too, and inch by inch
      Disputes the Lord's dominions—do not flinch,
      Nor for a moment think our work is done,
      'Till every see and parish are our own.

Mr Achmuty
      If, as you hope, we have secured the throne,
      We know the Chancellor will be our own.

Mr Jay *(earnestly)*
      My Lord! the fervour of your holy zeal,
      With the Lord's aid, may work on Mr Peel.[3]

Rev^d Mr Shumm
      I, as an humble servant of the Lord,
      Would take the smallest cure and labour hard.
      I am the greatest sinner upon earth,
      But wait his time to bring my glory forth.

Rev^d Mr Busby
      No work so lowly but what I would do,
      My gracious Lord, and deem it honour too.
      My sins are scarlet, yet I joy to know,
      My stedfast faith can wash them white as snow.

Mr Aimwell
      The talents that I have I would not hide;
      They are the Lord's, and I would have them tried,
      He will be tender to my sinful soul
      For I am his, and act by his control.
              (The Bishop bows to each.)

Mr Fripp

My gracious Lord, would you not deem it right,
As one manoeuvre of our holy fight,
To mix a few of our most able friends
With Bartlet's buildings?[4] for our godly ends
Cannot be fully answered, till we rule
With sway unlimited through church and school.

Bishop

The suggestion does you honour, my dear sir,
But it is ticklish ground—and ere we stir
The drowsy lions of that hostile den,
We must take care to pick and chuse our men.
Our funds look well—

Mr Fripp   Indeed, my lord, they do,
And much of this success we owe to you,
My Lady. The account that I have here
Shews what your several plans produced last year,
And I would wish, if I may be allow'd,
To read the Precious document aloud.

(All bow.)

Miss Fripp *(reads)*

Twopence a week paid by each private pew[5]
In Doctor Cantwell's chapel, one pound two;
Tracks on faith, not said how many
Sold by six beggars, sixteen and a penny.
From Harweall workhouse by a farthing rate,
Collected by myself, is one pound eight.
Crumbs for the Lord from door to door
Through Huntingdon, nineteen pound four.
From twelve old ladies, offrings from the hive,
In various sums amounts to one pound five.
From the new Sunday school as the Lord's fee,
By pennys from each child makes one pound three,
"The desperate Sinner's certain road to heaven,"
Sold at the gallows foot, brought one pound seven.
Offrings from all the 'lect who pick up sticks,
A penny for each bundle, one pound six.

A fine I've fixed on all the serious men
Seen smoking pipes amounts to one pound ten.

Mr Achmuty

Oh! this is noble!—Lady, zeal like this,
Palms of eternal glory cannot miss,
Plans such as these, through every county tried,
Will bring in much, which if with skill applied,
Will give us power in time to work our way.

Bishop

Aye, my dear Sir—how far no man can say,
From little causes great effects will spring,
We must not heed the snares that sinners fling.

(A short pause in the conversation; tea is again handed round.)

Achmuty, my dear friend, there was much grace,
In these few words, which lately in his place,
A wealthy member of your house let fall;
I cannot doubt but he will have a call—
He must be looked to—and that worthy man,
Who never fails to help us all he can,
Might he not, think you, change his line of trade?
In the Lord's cause much progress might be made,
If Mr Butterworth,[6] instead of acts,
Would take to sell only religious tracts.

Mr Achmuty

The thought is excellent my Lord,—and I
Will urge him instantly the plan to try;
Backed by your Lordship's name, I cannot doubt,
But all his law books will be soon turned out.

Mr Wilson *(suddenly addressing the Bishop)*

My Lord! will you with christian frankness tell,
If you still think, that I shall go to Hell?

Bishop *(no way surprised at his abruptness)*

I will not now so positively say,
As when I met you, Sir, the other day,
You then spoke much of virtue, much of works,
And in such jargon, danger always lurks.
But I have hope, now that I see you're found,
Where grace and faith so plenteously abound.

Mr Wilson

> The Lord be thanked! Indeed I'm much perplexed
> To know my chance of being damned or blessed.
> With all my power I labour not to sin,
> But that, I'm told, don't signify a pin.
> Indeed, my Lord, I never rest at night,
> But a cold sweat comes over me with fright,
> While thinking of the burning pains of Hell,
> Which we must all deserve—since Adam fell.

Bishop

> Such thoughts are wholesome, be assured, young man.
> And must be pleasing to God's blessed lamb.

Mr Combe (*starting up, and speaking with vehemence*)

> Hold! Hold! blasphemer!—poor bespotted youth,
> Learn in his works to know the God of truth.
> Did he, who for thy feet cool verdure spread,
> And arched his azure vault above thy head,
> He, who has left no sense without its joy,
> Did he create thee only to destroy?
> Leave, leave with me, these worse than fools, who dare—

Mr Jay (*seizing upon him in violent agitation*)

> Sweet Mr Edward Combe—beware! beware!
> What would your worthy pious father say?

Mr Combe

> I know not—care not Sir—but come what may,
> I will not stay to hear my God blasphemed.

Mrs Fripp

> Oh! let the monster go! we shall be deemed
> Too lost for grace, if more such words we hear.

Bishop

> *He* is, alas, too lost for grace I fear!
> And everlasting fire must be his fate,
> A fit abode for one so reprobate.
> Let us, my fellow sinners, all to prayer—
> And may the Lord's grace wash us from all share,
> In the transgressions of this hell-damned boy!

(*All the ladies and gentlemen kneel down, and John kneels down too.*)

Mr Combe
> This christian office shall have no alloy
> From me—my prayers might your hot ardour chill,
> I'll hie me to my chambers—and be still.

(All groan.)

F I N I S

NOTES

ALLEGRA
(pages 3-18)

[1] *The Works of Lord Byron: Letters and Journals*, ed. Rowland E. Prothero (London: John Murray, 1898-1901), III, 429.

[2] Claire's paternity is unknown; she may have been illegitimate. No record of her birth (believed to have taken place April 27, 1798) has been found. Her mother married Godwin twice on December 21, 1801, once as Mary Clairmont, once as Mary Vial. For details see Marion Kingston Stocking, "Introduction," *The Journals of Claire Clairmont* (Cambridge: Harvard University Press, 1968), pp. 13-15.

[3] *Letters and Journals*, III, 430, 435-36.

[4] Ralph Milbanke Lovelace, *Astarte: A Fragment of the Truth Concerning George Gordon Byron, Sixth Lord Byron*, ed. Mary Countess of Lovelace (London: Christophers, 1921), p. 267 (Letter of September 8, 1816).

[5] Leslie A. Marchand, *Byron: A Biography* (New York: Knopf, 1957), II, 681 (Letter of January 20, 1817).

[6] *The Letters of Percy Bysshe Shelley*, ed. Frederick L. Jones (Oxford: Clarendon Press, 1964), I, 529 (Letter of January 17, 1817).

[7] *Ibid.*, I, 539.

[8] *Letters and Journals*, IV, 123-24 (Letter of May 27, 1817).

[9] *The Letters of Percy Bysshe Shelley*, I, 584 (Letter of December 17, 1817).

[10] Marchand, II, 752-53 (Letter of November 11, 1818).

[11] *Lord Byron's Correspondence*, ed. John Murray (London: John Murray, 1922), II, 65 (Letter of January 13, 1818).

[12] *Lord Byron's Correspondence*, II, 71 (Letter of March 25, 1818).

[13] *Letters and Journals*, IV, 249-50 (Letter of August 3, 1818).

[14] *Astarte*, pp. 294-95 (Letter of September [?10], 1819).

[15] Iris Origo, *The Last Attachment: The Story of Byron and Teresa Guiccioli* (New York: Scribners, [1949]), p. 142.

[16] *Byron: A Self-Portrait: Letters and Diaries 1798 to 1824*, ed. Peter Quennell (London: John Murray, 1950), II, 510 (Letter to Richard Hoppner, March 31, 1820).

[17] Newman Ivey White elaborated the theory that Shelley had adopted the child, probably in the hope that it would compensate Mary for the loss of her daughter Clara, *Shelley* (New York: Knopf, 1940), II, 71-83. More recent scholars reject this explanation and consider Shelley the father of Elena, though not by Claire. Richard Holmes, following an explanation set forth by Ursula Orange in 1955, believes Elena the daughter of Shelley by Elise, *Shelley: The Pursuit* (London: Weidenfeld and Nicolson, 1974), pp. 465-74.

[18] *Letters and Journals*, VI, 99 (Letter of August 3, 1822).

[19] *Letters and Journals*, V, 14-15 (Letter of April 22, 1820).

[20] *Ibid.*, V, 74-75 (Letter of September 10, 1820).

[21] *Ibid.*, V, 262-64 (Letter of April 3, 1821).

[22] *Letters of Percy Bysshe Shelley*, II, 283 (Letter of April 16 [for 17], 1821).

[23] *Ibid.*, II, 334-35 (Letter of August 15, 1821).

[24] *Ibid.*, II, 338.

[25] Manuscript letter published by courtesy of the Pierpont Morgan Library. The Mother Superior's letter to Byron is dated September 28, 1821.

[26] Thomas Moore, *Letters and Journals of Lord Byron: with Notices of His Life* (London: John Murray, 1830), II, 615.

[27] Iris Origo, "Allegra," in *A Measure of Love* (London: Jonathan Cape, 1957), p. 80.

[28] *Letters and Journals*, VI, 53-54 (Letter of April 23, 1822).

[29] *Ibid.*, VI, 56-57 (Letter of May 4, 1822).

[30] Quennell, II, 694 (Letter of May 11, 1822).

[31] *The Letters of Percy Bysshe Shelley*, II, 415.

[32] Leslie A. Marchand, *Byron: A Portrait* (New York: Knopf, 1970), p. 373.

[33] Origo, *The Last Attachment*, p. 312.

HARROW

(pages 18-25)

[1] *Letters and Journals*, V, 445 ("Detached Thoughts," 72, October, 1821); see also V. 122: "When I went up to Trinity, in 1805, at the age of seventeen and a half, I was miserable and untoward to a degree. I was wretched at leaving Harrow, to which I had become attached during the last two years of my stay there" (Letter to John Murray, November 19, 1820).

[2] *Ibid.*, V, 463 ("Detached Thoughts," 113, November 5, 1821).

[3] *Ibid.*, VI, 50-52 (Letter of April 22, 1822).

[4] *Ibid.*, VI, 69-72 (Letter of May 26, 1822).

[5] Samuel Smiles, *A Publisher and His Friends: Memoir and Correspondence of John Murray* (London: John Murray, 1891), I, 430-31.

[6] *Ibid.*, I, 431.

[7] Letter of December 12, 1822, quoted from Doris Langley Moore, *Lord Byron: Accounts Rendered* (London: John Murray, 1974), p. 331. Miss Moore writes in detail of Byron's refusal to pay exorbitant embalming costs for Allegra, pp. 313-31.

[8] *Letters and Journals*, VI, 152-54. The material from "Cunningham is" through "the same Coward" was withheld by Prothero and is published here by permission of John Murray.

MRS. TROLLOPE

(pages 25-39)

[1] Anthony Trollope, *An Autobiography*, ed. Frederick Page (London: Oxford University Press, 1950), p. 2.

[2] Guglielmo Pepe, *Memoirs of General Pepe*, Written by Himself (London: Bentley, 1846), III, 270.

[3] Thomas Hamilton, *Men and Manners in America* (Philadelphia: Carey, Lea, & Blanchard, 1833), p. 293.

[4] Frances Eleanor Trollope, *Frances Trollope: Her Life and Literary Work* (London: Bentley, 1895), I, 150.

[5] *Ibid.*, I, 152-53.

[6] *Ibid.*, I, 151.

[7] Thomas Adolphus Trollope, *What I Remember* (New York: Harper, 1888), p. 161.

[8] *The Quarterly Review*, 47 (March, 1832), 39, 56, 58, 62, 80.

[9] *The Edinburgh Review*, 110 (July, 1832), 487, 481, 510, 496.

[10] Quoted from Michael Sadleir, *Trollope: A Commentary*, 3rd ed. (London: Oxford University Press, 1961), pp. 85-86.

[11] *What I Remember*, p. 182.

[12] *An Autobiography*, p. 29.

[13] *What I Remember*, p. 62.

[14] Charles Merivale, *Autobiography of Dean Merivale*, ed. Judith Anne Merivale (London: Edward Arnold, 1899), p. 31.

[15] *What I Remember*, pp. 62-63.

[16] *Ibid.*, pp. 63-64.

[17] *Ibid.*, p. 65.

[18] Sadleir, pp. 57-58.

[19] Frances Eleanor Trollope, I, 92.

[20] *Ibid.*, I, 204.

[21] Thomas Adolphus requested Trollope's son Henry to send him the manuscript "about Cunningham of Harrow having spoken to Harry Drury about Byron's Cain with the answer he got from Drury" (Letter of Dec. 13, 1886, University of Illinois Library).

[22] *What I Remember*, p. 64.

[23] *An Autobiography*, p. 22.

[24] Donald Smalley, "Introduction," to *Domestic Manners of the Americans* (New York: Random House, 1949), p. xli.

[25] For a discussion of the continuations and imitations of *Don Juan*, see Samuel Chew, *Byron in England: His Fame and After-Fame* (New York: Scribners, 1924), chap. v.

[26] For a brief discussion of Byron's *ottava rima*, see Leslie A. Marchand, *Byron's Poetry: A Critical Introduction* (Cambridge: Harvard University Press, 1968), pp. 145-49.

[27] *An Autobiography*, p. 21.

ANTHONY TROLLOPE

(pages 39-49)

[1] *An Autobiography*, pp. 1 and 71.

[2] *Ibid.*, p. 4.

[3] *Ibid.*, pp. 5-6.

[4] *Ibid.*, p. 9.

[5] *Ibid.*, pp. 11-12.

[6] Sir William Gregory, *An Autobiography*, ed. Lady Gregory (London: John Murray, 1894), p. 35.

[7] Trollope, *An Autobiography*, pp. 16-17.

[8] *Ibid.*, pp. 17-18.

9 *Ibid.*, p. 28.

10 Smiles, II, 384.

11 *Family Memorials,* ed. Anna W. Merivale (Exeter: privately printed, 1884), p. 238.

12 Frances Eleanor Trollope, I, 180-81.

13 T.H.S. Escott, *Anthony Trollope: His Public Services, Private Friends and Literary Originals* (London: John Lane, 1913), p. 29.

14 Percy M. Thornton, *Harrow School and its Surroundings* (London: W. H. Allen, 1885), p. 250.

15 *The Letters of Anthony Trollope,* ed. Bradford Allen Booth (London: Oxford University Press, 1951), p. 1.

16 *An Autobiography,* p. 42.

17 *Ibid.*, p. 52.

18 *Ibid.*, pp. 21-22.

19 *What I Remember,* p. 491.

20 *An Autobiography,* p. 41.

21 *The New Zealander,* ed. N. John Hall (Oxford: Clarendon Press, 1972), p. 174.

22 A list of Trollope's outloud reading was published in *Notes and Queries* for March, 1975.

AFTERWARDS

(pages 49-54)

1 Julius Millingen, *Memoirs of the Affairs of Greece. . . . With Various Anecdotes Relating to Lord Byron* (London: J. Rodwell, 1831), p. 100.

2 Edward Williams' Diary for May 6, 1822, quoted in Thomas Love Peacock, *Memoirs of Shelley,* ed. Howard Mills (New York: New York University Press, 1970), p. 79.

3 *The Letters of Mary W. Shelley,* ed. Frederick L. Jones (Norman: University of Oklahoma Press, 1944), II, 81 and 88 (Letters to Maria Gisborne, July 17 and October 30, 1834).

4 Ethel Colburn Mayne, *The Life and Letters of Anne Isabella, Lady Byron* (London: Constable, 1929), p. 331.

5 R. Glynn Grylls, *Claire Clairmont, Mother of Byron's Allegra* (London: John Murray, 1939), Appendix C, p. 266.

6 Herbert Huscher, "Claire Clairmont's Lost Russian Journal and Some Further Glimpses of Her Later Life," *Keats-Shelley Memorial Bulletin,* 6 (1955), 47.

7 *The Notebooks of Henry James,* ed. F. O. Matthiessen and Kenneth Murdock (New York: Oxford University Press, 1947), p. 72.

8 *Autobiography of Dean Merivale,* p. 32.

9 *The Christian Observer,* 60 (November, 1861), 885.

10 *The New Monthly Magazine,* 55 (March, 1839), 417.

11 *An Autobiography,* p. 17.

12 Unsigned review of *Orley Farm, The National Review,* 16 (January, 1863), 28.

13 *The Last Chronicle of Barset,* chap. xlvii.

LINES WRITTEN BY A CELEBRATED AUTHORESS
ON THE BURIAL OF THE
DAUGHTER OF A CELEBRATED AUTHOR
(pages 55-76)

[1] Nowhere in the manuscript does Anthony Trollope mention his mother by name; the book referred to is *Domestic Manners of the Americans* (1832).

[2] In his liberal youth Robert Southey had written *Wat Tyler*, a revolutionary dramatic poem (1794); its unauthorized publication in 1817 greatly embarrassed Southey, then Poet Laureate and staunch conservative.

[3] George D'Oyly, D.D. (1778-1846), Rector of Lambeth and Sundridge. He published various collections of sermons, collaborated on a very popular *Annotated Bible* (1814), and contributed regularly to Murray's *Quarterly Review*.

[4] *Letters and Journals*, VI, 78, 121, 132, 138. See also *Medwin's Conversations with Lord Byron*, ed. Ernest J. Lovell, Jr. (Princeton: Princeton University Press, 1966), p. 155.

[5] This line evidently had been lost or deleted from the copy from which Trollope worked.

[6] Rev. Henry ("Harry") Joseph Thomas Drury (1778-1841).

[7] Space blank in Trollope's manuscript.

[8] In fact the lines are plainly intelligible as written; Trollope's "correction" would badly throw off the meter. The same may be said for his interpolations in stanzas 35 and 36, below.

[9] Harry Drury was an ardent bibliophile and an original member of the famous Roxburghe Club (founded London, 1812). His mania for collecting expensive volumes was probably the leading cause of his bankruptcy in 1827.

[10] Perhaps Mrs. Trollope herself is the "certain poet."

[11] Rev. Benjamin Evans (ca. 1770-1833), third master at Harrow School in 1822; made under master in 1826.

[12] Rev. William Mills (1788-1854), sixth master at Harrow School and subsequently Headmaster of Exeter Grammar School and Rector of St. Paul's, Exeter. Thomas Henry Baylis, Q.C., who was a classmate of Trollope at Harrow during the 1830's, recalled that Trollope "fought with a boy of the name of Lewis in the fighting-ground for nearly an hour, until separated by Mills the master." Baylis probably refers to the fight which Trollope in his *Autobiography* called the "solitary glory of my schooldays." E. W. Howson and G. T. Warner, *Harrow School* (London: E. Arnold, 1898), p. 80.

[13] *shell*: an intermediate class between numbered forms (the term originally derived from the shape of the end of the schoolroom at Westminster School). The "shell" at Harrow during Trollope's time was described by a schoolmate as "a kind of limbo between the fourth and fifth forms," itself divided into lower and upper shell, of which the latter "was composed of extremely big and extremely ignorant boys." Sir William Gregory, *An Autobiography*, p. 30.

14 Rev. Samuel Ellis Batten (1792-1830), seventh master.

15 Rev. Benjamin Hall Kennedy (1804-89), assistant master at Harrow and subsequently Headmaster of Shrewsbury, Regius Professor of Greek at Cambridge, and Canon of Ely. The Harrow boarding house referred to was known as "The Grove."

16 Rev. William James Joseph Drury (ca. 1797-1878), fifth master.

17 Rev. Mark Drury (ca. 1763-1835), under master at Harrow until 1826. It was in this year that Mark and William, in debt for an alleged forty thousand pounds, fled their creditors. Trollope served briefly in the summer of 1834 as a classical usher in William Drury's school at Brussels.

18 Rev. George Butler (1774-1853), Headmaster of Harrow School, 1805-29, and subsequently Dean of Peterborough.

19 While Butler was headmaster, enrollment at Harrow sank from nearly 300 to 128; it is less than fair, however, to ascribe the decline to Butler's "inefficiency."

20 Anne Isabella Milbanke (1792-1860), Byron's estranged wife.

21 *Blackwoods* 11 (January, 1822), 91; *Gentleman's Magazine* 91 (December, 1821), 613; *Edinburgh Review* 36 (February, 1822), 437; *The Letters of Percy Bysshe Shelley*, II, 388 (Letter to John Gisborne, January 26, 1822).

22 Campbell is doubtless the same person whom Guglielmo Pepe in a letter to Mrs. Trollope of January 9, 1825 calls "our excellent friend Mr. Campbell" Frances Eleanor Trollope, I, 43. Trollope had in mind, among other financial "smashes," that of his own family in 1834, of Harry Drury in 1827, and of Mark and William Drury in 1826.

OTHER POEMS
IN ANTHONY TROLLOPE'S "SALMAGUNDI"
(pages 77-82)

1 *The Letters of Thomas Moore*, ed. Wilfred S. Dowden (Oxford: Clarendon Press, 1964), I, 319-20.

2 Lady Sydney Morgan, *Lady Morgan's Memoirs* (London: W. H. Allen, 1862), II, 200.

3 Mabell, Countess of Airlie, *In Whig Society, 1775-1818* (London: Hodder and Stoughton, 1921), pp. 151-52.

4 *Letters and Journals*, IV, 12 (Letter to Thomas Moore, Dec. 5, 1816).

5 *White's*: famous club in St. James Street, noted as a gaming house; its membership was decidedly aristocratic and Tory. The fête in celebration of the victory over Napoleon was held June 20, 1814.

6 Queen (actually Princess) Caroline, estranged wife of the Prince Regent.

7 *Carlton House*: the Regent's London residence.

8 The *Morning Chronicle* had an asterisk footnote here: "Like Louis *le bien-aimé*, Louis *le desiré*, &c. &c."

APPENDIX
MRS. TROLLOPE'S ANTI-EVANGELICAL VERSE DRAMA
(pages 83-94)

[1] In her anti-evangelical novel *The Vicar of Wrexhill* (1837), Mrs. Trollope has a character "compose" these very ten lines after examining an evangelical album; only slight changes were effected: "Here's the bower" for "Fly not yet" and "maiden" for "virgin" (II, 141).

[2] Francesco Redi (1626-96), Italian poet, scientist, and philologist. Although Redi's best-known work was a dithyramb, *Bacco in Toscano*, he also wrote sonnets.

[3] Robert Peel (1788-1850), most important Tory/Conservative leader of his day.

[4] Perhaps a reference to William Henry Bartlett (1809-54) and his drawings for John Britton's *Cathedral Antiquities of England* (1814-32).

[5] In *The Vicar of Wrexhill*, one of Mrs. Trollope's heroines, after examining the record book of a seller of evangelical tracts, composes a poem; changes in the published version include "Cartwright" for "Cantwell," "Wrexhill workhouse" for "Harweal workhouse," "Hampshire" for "Huntingdon" (II, 272).

[6] Henry Butterworth (1786-1860), whose well-known law publishing firm, founded in 1816, is still in existence today.

INDEX

This book, SALMAGUNDI, has been published
in an edition of two thousand copies.
The text was composed in Linotype Baskerville
and printed on Warren's Old Style Wove paper
at the Princeton University Press.
The plates are by the
Meriden Gravure Company of Meriden, Connecticut,
the format by P. J. Conkwright.